全国考研辅导班教材系列

2011年
考研英语
写作突破100题

（英语一、英语二适用）

2011 Nian Kaoyan Yingyu Xiezuo Tupo 100 Ti

● 宫东风英语教学团队

高等教育出版社·北京
HIGHER EDUCATION PRESS　BEIJING

U0062939

图书在版编目（CIP）数据

2011 年考研英语写作突破 100 题／宫东风英语教学团队编写. —北京：高等教育出版社, 2010.3

英语一、二适用

ISBN 978－7－04－028777－6

Ⅰ.①2… Ⅱ.①宫… Ⅲ.①英语－写作－研究生－入学考试－自学参考资料　Ⅳ.①H315

中国版本图书馆 CIP 数据核字（2010）第 038592 号

策划编辑	刘　佳	**责任编辑**	杨挺扬	**封面设计**	王凌波
版式设计	马敬茹	**责任校对**	杨凤玲	**责任印制**	韩　刚

出版发行	高等教育出版社	**购书热线**	010－58581118	
社　　址	北京市西城区德外大街 4 号	**免费咨询**	400－810－0598	
邮政编码	100120	**网　　址**	http://www.hep.edu.cn	
总　　机	010－58581000		http://www.hep.com.cn	
		网上订购	http://www.landraco.com	
			http://www.landraco.com.cn	
经　　销	蓝色畅想图书发行有限公司	**畅想教育**	http://www.widedu.com	
印　　刷	高等教育出版社印刷厂			
开　　本	787×1092　1/16	**版　　次**	2010 年 3 月第 1 版	
印　　张	13.5	**印　　次**	2010 年 3 月第 1 次印刷	
字　　数	320 000	**定　　价**	22.00 元	

本书如有缺页、倒页、脱页等质量问题，请到所购图书销售部门联系调换。

版权所有　侵权必究

物料号　28777－00

前　　言

　　教育部每年颁布的《英语考试大纲》明确规定和解释了两个写作任务：应用文写作和短文写作。其中，应用文写作占总分的10%；短文写作分别占英语（一）和英语（二）总分的20%和15%。这两个写作任务总计英语（一）30分；英语（二）25分。这一点足以证明写作在考研英语中的重要性。实际上，考生们也都十分重视写作，将其视为征服考研英语的重中之重。目前，考生们正在选择不同的书籍和方法提高写作能力。当然，"开卷有益"是一个不可争议的事实。但是，考生的有效复习时间是极其有限的，这一现实迫使每一位励志成功的考生必须寻找到一种多快好省的方法来提高写作能力。实践证明：精研熟背经典范文和模板是短期内迅速提高写作能力的高效方法之一，因为经典范文和模板涵盖了考研大纲对高分作文所要求的精美词句和命题内容。

　　本书编写目的：

　　1. 使考生在最短的时间内了解并且掌握考研大纲在写作方面的要求与标准，全面提升考研复习的速度。

　　2. 解决广大考生目前的一个常见问题：面对考题，没有写作思路，不知道写什么，写多少，怎么写。

　　3. 解决一些同学的写作难题：知道用中文怎么写，但是不知道如何用英文把自己的思想表达出来。

　　4. 通过精研熟背本书的范文和模板，牢固掌握考研英语写作的实用应试方法。

　　本书具体特色：

　　1. 涵盖最新内容，紧扣大纲重点和考点。

　　本书共收录了100篇经典范文和模板。其中，应用文写作和短文写作各50篇。精研熟背了本书中的100篇经典范文和模板就等于掌握了大纲的核心内容。

　　2. 适当扩充要点词汇，全面提高写作能力。

　　本书对大纲中的要点词汇进行了适当的扩充和运用，以帮助考生系统地提高写作能力。这样可以切实可行地夯实考生的基础，使考生充满自信地面对考研写作试题。

　　3. 遵循命题规律，扫清写作障碍。

　　本书根据大纲要求，尤其是历年命题规律，精选了100篇经典范文。每篇文章均贴近考点、难点和知识点，使复习范围与考试范围相一致。

　　4. 写作原文和译文全面翔实，中英文对照加强语感。

　　本书为100篇经典范文和模板提供了详细准确的译文，以便考生能够深刻并且准确地牢记写作所涉及的每一个单词和句子结构。

　　本书使用建议：

　　1. 每天至少保证一篇经典范文和模板的学习量，循环往复，一直坚持到年底，因为"天道酬勤"。

2. 先从本书的应用文入手，因为这部分比较简单。

3. 学习每篇经典范文与模板时，首先将重点词语点睛部分朗读一至三遍。然后，对写作要求和英语原文进行通读。

4. 通读之后，考生应该针对经典范文与模板进行逐句精读。具体精读方法是：读一句英文读一句汉语。这样读有利于记住重点词句。

5. 精读之后，如时间允许，每天抄写精读的经典范文与模板，因为常言道："好脑子不如烂笔头"。

6. 在第二轮精研本书 100 篇经典范文与模板时，一定要付出更大的努力，除了达到上述的要求外，还要背诵默写，因为只有这样做，才能把写作知识变成自己的能力。

7. 考生研读本书时一定要保持一种好心情，因为态度决定一切。

众所周知：学而不思则无获。只要同学们多一种学习方法，就会多一份成功的希望。当你学完本书时，你一定会向着更高的写作高峰发起进攻。愿本书照亮你的写作之路！Nothing is impossible to a willing heart. Keep on moving. You are the best!

本书编者
2010 年 2 月

目　　录

第一部分 考研英语写作与对策

研究生入学考试英语（一）和（二）的写作部分分别占总分的 30% 和 25%，是决定考研英语成绩优劣的重要因素。因此考生需要认真理解、领会考研英语写作的每个细节，并且尽快掌握相应的应试对策，以便在考试最后的一个小时能够合理地控制时间（小作文 20~25 分钟，大作文 30~35 分钟），从容地完成较高质量的写作。

一、大纲对写作的界定与最新评分细则

写作是全国硕士研究生入学考试英语试卷的第三部分。该部分考查考生的书面表达能力，共 2 节，30 分（英语二是 25 分）。在 A 节中，考生根据所给情景写出一篇约 100 词（标点符号不计算在内）的应用性短文，包括私人和公务信函、摘要、报告、备忘录等。考生在答题卡 2 上作答。总分 10 分。在 B 节中，考生根据提示信息写出一篇 160~200 词的短文（英语二要求 150 词以上，标点符号不计算在内）。提示信息的形式有主题句、写作提纲、规定情景、图、表等。考生在答题卡 2 上作答，总分 20 分（英语二总分为 15 分）。

1. 大纲对写作的界定

《全国硕士研究生入学统一考试英语考试大纲（非英语专业）（2011 年版）》在考试说明部分对写作有如下界定：

考生应能写不同类型的应用文，包括私人和公务信函、备忘录、摘要、报告等，还应能写一般描述性、叙述性、说明性或议论性的文章。写作时，考生应能：

（1）做到语法、拼写、标点正确，用词恰当；

（2）遵循文章的特定文体格式；

（3）合理组织文章结构，使其内容统一、连贯；

（4）根据写作目的和特定读者，恰当选用语域。

2. 最新考研英语写作具体评分细则

第五档　（A 节 9~10 分；英语一 B 节 17~20 分，英语二 B 节 13~15 分）

内容切题，包括题中所列的各项内容，清楚表达其内涵，文字连贯；句式有变化，句子结构和用词正确。文章长度符合要求。

第四档　（A 节 7~8 分；英语一 B 节 13~16 分，英语二 B 节 10~12 分）

内容切题，包括题中所列的各项内容；比较清楚地表达其内涵，文字基本连贯，句式有一定变化，句子结构和用词无重大错误。文章长度符合要求。

第三档　（A 节 5~6 分；英语一 B 节 9~12 分，英语二 B 节 7~9 分）

内容切题，基本包括题中所列各方面的内容；基本清楚地表达其内涵；句子结构和词有少量错误。文章长度符合要求。

第二档　（A 节 3~4 分；英语一 B 节 5~8 分，英语二 B 节 4~6 分）

内容基本切题，基本包含题中所列各方面的内容；语句可以理解，文章长度基本符合要求。

第一档 （A节1~2分；英语一B节1~4分，英语二B节1~3分）

基本按要求写作，但只有少数句子可以理解。

零档 （0分）

文不切题，语句混乱，无法理解。

二、考研英语写作的高分标准

考研英语写作的高分标准涉及以下六个方面：

（1）内容切题。审题准，不跑题。文不对题会严重影响成绩，导致写作失败。

（2）表达清楚。语言要简洁、准确、条理清晰，主题明确。

（3）意义连贯。遣词造句得当，表达连贯平稳。论点论据展开合理（以因果、对比、分类、定义、列举、概括、详情、时间、空间、过程或综合等方法来展开）。

（4）句式有变化。采用适当的句式来表达相应的内容。常用句式包括简单句、并列句、复合句、主被动句、长句、短句、否定句、双重否定句、疑问句、反问句、倒装句、强调句、插入语、独立主格成分等。

（5）用词有变化。避免重复使用同一词汇，可适当使用代词、同义词、近义词、关联词使表达富有动感。同义词的使用是衡量考生语言运用能力的一个尺度。

（6）语言规范。符合英语的表达习惯，语法错误少，写出的英语不是中式英语。

三、历届考研英语写作命题与启示

1. 历届考研英语写作命题总览

考试年代	考试题目	选题范围
1991 年	WHERE TO LIVE—IN THE CITY OR THE COUNTRY?	环境
1992 年	FOR A BETTER UNDERSTANDING BETWEEN PARENT AND CHILD	子女教育
1993 年	ADVERTISEMENT ON TV	传媒
1994 年	ON MAKING FRIENDS	人际交往
1995 年	THE "PROJECT HOPE"	教育
1996 年	GOOD HEALTH	健康
1997 年	SMOKING	健康
1998 年	BUSINESS PROMISE & GUARANTEE	诚信
1999 年	HUMAN POPULATION & WILDLIFE PROTECTION	环境
2000 年	WORLD COMMERCIAL FISHING	环境
2001 年	LOVE	人际关系
2002 年	CULTURE—NATIONAL AND INTERNATIONAL	文化

考试年代	考试题目	选题范围
2003 年	THE FLOWER IN THE GREENHOUSE CAN NOT WITHSTAND THE ORDEAL OF WIND AND STORM	子女教育
2004 年	THE END IS ALSO A NEW START	人生
2005 年	A "FOOTBALL MATCH" OF TAKING CARE OF PARENTS	道德
2006 年	THE BLIND WORSHIP OF STARS	青年思想教育
2007 年	SELF-CONFIDENCE AND BRAVERY	青年心理问题
2008 年	MUTUAL HELP AND COOPERATION	人生教育
2009 年	NETWORK AND DISTANCE	网络的影响力
2010 年	"CULTURAL HOT POT"	中外文化交流

2. 历届考研英语写作试题类型

历届考研英语写作试题主要分为以下两大类型：

（1）1991—1996 年：给出提纲或开头句的命题写作（writings based on given outlines or opening sentences）

（2）1997—2010 年：给出提纲的图画或图表写作（writings based on visual information or pictures or graphs）

3. 历届考研英语写作命题的启示

从 1991—2010 年共计 20 年的考题来分析，我们可以对考研英语写作命题有如下认识：

（1）写作题目忌偏忌怪。考研英语写作选题范围都是目前人们最为关注的问题，从子女与父母的关系到健康的重要性，从近年来泛滥的行业"承诺"到世界烟民的现状、从希望工程到电视广告、从环境保护到生物种类趋于灭绝，以及 2008 年、2009 年和 2010 年的考题所涉及的互助合作、网络作用以及中外文化交流的题目，无不反映了当前社会的热门话题。

（2）文体基本上是说明文和议论文。考这类体裁的写作比较符合形势发展的实际需要。在学习、工作和生活中，人们所书写的材料大多也是说明文或议论文。

（3）出题形式在平稳中逐渐趋于多样化。2005 年考研新增加了应用短文写作。

（4）写作题目易于理解。写作题目无论以文字的形式还是以图表、图画的形式出现都浅显易懂。考生不会因题目中出现生词或难以理解的短语而影响正常发挥。

四、考研英语写作的常规整体构建模式

考研英语短文写作的文章一般包括一个开头段、若干扩展段和一个结尾段。开头段和结尾段一般比扩展段短。各种段落的作用、特点和写作方法如下所示。

1. 开头段

开头段一定要语言精练，并且直接切入主题。开头段一般不对主题进行深入的探讨，具体的论证或叙述应该在扩展段进行。一般在开头段写四、五句即可。考生应注意以下若干要点：

（1）开头段的作用

概括陈述主题，提出观点或论点，表明写作意图。

（2）写开头段时考生应该避免的若干问题

① 开头偏离主题太远；

② 使用抱歉或埋怨之类的词句；

③ 内容不具体，言之无物；

④ 使用不言自明的陈述。

（3）开头段的表达方法

① 使用引语（use a quotation）

使用一段名人名言或人们常用的谚语、习语，以确定文章的写作范围和方向。

例：

"Great minds must be ready not only to take the opportunity, but to make them." Colton, a great writer once remarked. But it still has a profound significance now. To a person, in whose lifetime opportunities are not many, to make opportunities is more essential to his success.

② 使用具体翔实的数字或数据（use figures or statistics）

引用一些具体翔实的数字或数据，然后做出概括性分析，指明问题的症结所在。

例：

In the past 5 years there has been a marked decline in the number of young married couples who want to have children, coupled with a growing trend toward delayed childbearing. According to official statistics, in 2004, about 28 percent of married couples with wives under 35 gave no birth to children, compared with the 1994 level of 8 percent.

③ 提出问题（ask a question）

提出有争议或探讨性的具体问题，然后加以简要回答或展开引导性简短讨论。

例：

What do you want from your work? Money? Promotions? Interesting challenges? Continual learning? Work-based friendships? The opportunity to develop your own idea and potential? Though we are all individuals and so our answers will differ, all agree that work provides more than material things.

④ 给出背景（offer relevant background）

描述具体事件的时间、地点和发生背景等。

例：

Once in a newspaper I read of a crowd of people who remained appallingly indifferent to the plea of a mother. As she failed to offer the required amount of cash as a price to save her drowning son, the woman at last watched her son sink to death. The story is not rare in newspapers and on TV, and the casualness and detachment our people now have developed has aroused nationwide concern.

⑤ 定义法（give definition）

针对讨论的主题或问题加以定义，然后进行深入探讨。

例:

Flexibility is defined as being adaptable to change. In the course of your lifetime, it is essential that you learn to bend and flex around every new circumstance, as rigidity deprives you of the opportunity to see new possibilities. Paradigms change over time, and so must you. Your company may restructure, and you will have to survive. Your spouse may choose to leave the marriage, and you will have to cope. Technology will continue to advance and change, and you must constantly learn and adapt or risk becoming a dinosaur. Flexibility allows you to be ready for whatever curve lies ahead in life instead of getting blindsided by it.

⑥ 主题句法 (use of topic sentence)

文章一开始就以主题句点明全文主题, 然后围绕主题内容进行发展。

例:

Now people become increasingly aware of the importance of acquiring a mastery of a foreign language. To them, the knowledge of a foreign language, say, English, often means a good opportunity for one's career, even a passport to a prosperous future. Many of them equate success in life with the ability of speaking a foreign language.

(4) 开头段的常用核心句型

• The arguer may be right about …, but he seems to neglect (fail) to mention (take into account) the fact that …

• As opposed to (Contrary to) widely (commonly / generally) held (accepted) belief (ideas / views), I believe (argue) that …

• Although many people believe that …, I doubt (wonder) whether the argument bears much analysis (close examination).

• The advantages of B outweigh any benefit we gained from (carry more weight than those of / are much greater than) A.

• Although it is commonly (widely / generally) held (felt / accepted / agreed) that …, it is unlikely to be true that …

• There is an element of truth in this argument (statement), but it ignores a deeper and more basic (important / essential) fact (reason) that …

• It is true that (True, / To be sure, / Admittedly,) …, but this is not to say (it is unlikely / it doesn't follow / it doesn't mean / it won't be the case) that …

• The main (obvious / great) problem (flaw / drawback) with (in) this argument (view / remark) is that it is ignorant of (blind to) the basic (bare) fact that …

• It would be possible (natural / reasonable) to think (believe / take the view) that …, but it would be absurd (wrong) to claim (argue) that …

• In all the discussion and debate over …, one important (basic) fact is generally overlooked (neglected).

• There is absolutely (in fact) no (every) reason for us to believe (accept / resist / reject) that …

- Logical (Valid / Sound) as this argument and I wholeheartedly agree with it, it appears insignificant (absurd) when … is taken into consideration (account).

- To assume (suggest) that … is far from being proved (to miss the point).

- A close (careful) inspection (examination / scrutiny) of this argument would reveal how flimsy (groundless/fallacious) it is.

- On the surface (At first thought), it (this) may seem a sound (an attractive) suggestion (solution / idea), but careful weighing on the mind (on closer analysis / on second thought), we find that …

- Too much emphasis placed on (attention paid to / importance attached to) … may obscure (overlook / neglect) other facts …

- The danger (problem / fact / truth / point) is that …

- What the arguer fails to understand (consider / mention) is that …

- We don't have to look very far to see (find out) the truth (validity) of this argument (proposition).

- However just (logical / sound / valid) this argument may be, it only skims the surface of the problem.

- Among the most convincing (important) reasons given (cited / offered / identified) by people for …, one should be stressed (emphasized / mentioned).

- As far as I am concerned, however, I believe that …

- I believe that the title statement is valid because (of) …

- I agree with the above statement because I believe that …

- Although I appreciate that …, I cannot agree with the title statement.

- There is a public controversy nowadays over the issue of …Those who object to … argue that …But people who favor …, on the other hand, argue that …

- Currently (In recent years / In the past few years / For many years now), there is (has been) a general (widespread / growing / widely held) feeling towards (concern over / attitude towards / trend towards / awareness of / realization of / illusion of / belief in) …

- Now it is commonly (widely / generally / increasingly) believed (thought / held / accepted/ felt / recognized / acknowledged) that …But I wonder (doubt) whether …

- These days we are often told that (often hear about) …, but is this really the case?

2. 中间段

中间段是文章的正文，其作用是从不同的层面对文章主题进行具体和翔实的解释及论证。

(1) 中间段的一般特征

① 篇幅一般比开头段和结尾段长；

② 每段有相应的主题句；

③ 包含定义、解释、描写，说明主题思想的扩展句可以采用实例、数据或个人经历等写作手段；

④ 不同种类的段落采用不同的扩展手段。

（2）中间段的具体特点

① 所涉及内容应该准确、清楚，颇具说服力；

② 段落中一定具备主题句；

③ 段落内容应该保持完整、统一，没有说明不足之处或多余冗长的细节；

④ 内容顺序安排合理，逻辑性较强；

⑤ 段落之间连贯自然；

⑥ 段落中讨论的内容主次分明，材料比例适当；

⑦ 词与句型运用合理并且有变化。

（3）中间段展开的基本方法

① 列举法

例文：

There are a number of ways for us to keep fit. First, no matter how busy we are, we should have exercise every day to strengthen our muscles. Second, it is important to keep good hours. For example, if we are in the habit of going to bed early and getting up early, we can avoid overworking ourselves and get enough sleep. Finally, entertainment is also necessary so that we may have some moments of relaxation. If we follow those instruction, we will certainly be in good health.

② 比较对比法

例文：

The older form of communication is speech. In the beginning of human history, people could only use direct verbal speech to communicate. But it had many shortcomings. For instance, we could not speak to a person far away when we needed. So distance was a problem. And the spoken word could not be kept secret easily. So people wanted to invent a new method of communication. The next big step forward in communication was the invention of writing. Writing is one of human being's most important inventions. It solved the problem of distance and keeping secrets, but it too had disadvantages. The written word could not be passed on quickly, so people tried to find a new quicker method of communication.

The most recent development had been electronic means of communication, including the wireless telegraph, radio, telephone and television. The invention and use of electronic means has solved all the problems mentioned above. They are the most effective methods of communication. People will certainly try their best to invent even more modern and useful methods.

③ 因果法

例文：

The hamburger is the most popular food item in the United States. Every year Americans consume billions of them. They are sold in expensive restaurants and in humble diners. They are cooked at home on the kitchen stove or over a barbecue grill in the backyard. Why are they so popular?

First, a hamburger is extremely easy to prepare. It is nothing more than a piece of ground beef, cooked for a few minutes. Then it is placed in a sliced bun. Nothing could be simpler. Even an unskilled cook can turn out hundreds of them in an hour. Besides that, the simple hamburger can be varied in many ways. You can melt some cheese on top of the beef to create a cheeseburger. You can also add some grilled bacon for an interesting flavor contrast. In addition, you can garnish the hamburger with other things such as lettuce, tomato, onion, mushrooms, avocado, pickles, hot pepper, ketchup, relish, mayonnaise, mustard or whatever you wish!

④ 例证法

例文：

The saying "No pains, no gains" is universally accepted because of the plain yet philosophical moral it teaches: if one wants to achieve something, he has to work and tolerate more than others. The saying is true of any pursuit man seeks. A case in point is boxing. While we heap cheers on the winner, few happen to imagine that his gold belt is won at the cost of his sweat, tears, blood, even life over years before the arrival of that exciting moment.

⑤ 发展过程法

例文：

To build your own sunscope, get a carton and cut a hole in one side, big enough to poke your head through. Paste white paper on the inside surface that you will be facing. Then punch a pinhole into the opposite side high enough so that the little shaft of light will miss your head. For a sharper image you can make a better pinhole by cutting a one-inch square hole in the carton, taping a piece of aluminum foil over this hole, and then making the pinhole in the foil. Finally, tape the box shut and cover all light leaks with black tape.

⑥ 定义法

例文：

Diligence is the key to success. It means persistent work and does not mean that we are to exert ourselves all day and night without rest, without food and without sleep. The true meaning of diligence is the careful use of time for the purpose of improvement, or to work persistently without any waste of time.

⑦ 分类法

例文：

Nowadays the news media mainly consists of radio, television and newspapers. Each type has its own advantages and disadvantages.

Newspapers are the oldest form for communicating the news. Today many people still begin their day by reading the morning paper while having breakfast, and end their day by reading the evening paper while having dinner.

The invention of the radio has had a tremendous influence on the world. It is able to bring up-to-minute news to distant places in a matter of seconds. Thus the development of the radio has made the world a smaller place.

Television is the most recently developed device for communication. It allows us to see as well as to hear the news. The fact that it enables people to see visual images has had a considerable effect on our perceptions of world event.

（4）中间段的常用核心句型

• Although the popular belief is that …, a current（new / recent）study（survey / poll / investigation）indicates（shows / demonstrates）that …

• Common sense tells us that …

• The increase（change / failure / success）in …mainly（largely / partly）results from （arises from / is because of）…

• The increase（change / failure / success）in …is due to（owing to / attributable to） the fact that …

• Many people would claim that …

• One may attribute（ascribe / owe）the increase（decrease / change）to …but … is not by itself an adequate explanation.

• One of the reasons given for …is that …

• What is also worth noticing is that …

• There are many（different / several /a number of / a variety of）causes（reasons）for this dramatic（marked / significant）growth（change / decline / increase）in …

• There is no evidence to suggest that …

• Why are（is / do / did）…? For one thing, … For another, …

• Another reason why I dispute the above statement is that …

• It gives rise to（lead to / bring /create）a host of problems（consequences）.

• There are numerous reasons why …, and I shall here explore only a few of the most important ones.

• It will exert（have / produce）profound（far-reaching / remarkable / considerable / beneficial / favorable / undesirable / disastrous）effect（influence）on …

• A multitude of factors could account for（contribute to / lead to / result in / influence）the change（increase / decrease / success / failure / development）in …

• In 2009, it increased（rose / jumped / shot up）from 5 to 10 percent of the total（to 15 percent / by 15 percent）.

• By comparison with 2008, it decreased（dropped / fell）from 10 to 5 percent（to 15 percent / by 15 percent）.

• It accounts for 15 percent of the total.

• There were 100 traffic accidents in April, an increase of 5 percent in a five-month period.

• By 2010, only（less than / more than / almost / about / over/ as many as）three quarters（40 percent of / one out of five / one in four）college population（graduates / housewives) as against (as compared with) last year (2008) preferred to (liked) …

- With the development (improvement / rise / growth / general recognition / acknowledgement / realization) of …, vast changes awaits this country's society.

- Now people in growing (ever-increasing / significant) numbers are beginning (coming / getting) to believe (realize / recognize / understand / accept / see / be aware) that …

- According to a(n) recent (new / official) study (survey / report / poll), …

- History (Our society) is filled (abounds) with the examples of …

- The story (case / instance / situation) is not rare (isolated / unique), it is one of many examples (typical of dozens).

- A (one) recent (new / general / nationwide) study (survey / poll / investigation) conducted (taken) at a university by (officials / scientists / experts) indicates (reveals / suggests / shows / proves / demonstrates) that …

- According to (As can be seen in / As is shown in) the figures (statistics / findings / data / graph / table) released (provided) by the government (an institute), it can be learned (seen / predicted) that …

- There is (no) good (every / little / sufficient / considerable / strong) evidence (proof) to …

- Personal experience (Examples I heard / read of) leads me to conclude that …

- We must admit the undeniable fact that …

- No one can deny (ignore / doubt / overlook / obscure / brush aside) the fact that …

- Experience (Evidence) suggests (shows) that …

- Take for example … who (that) …

- The same is true of …

- As the saying goes, "…"

3. 结尾段

结尾段的写作方法可以归纳为下列若干种：

(1) 总结归纳

简要总结归纳文章要点，以便深化主题印象。

例：

In conclusion I would like to say that change is a problem confronting most of us today. The changes which have already taken place in every field of our life are irreversible. Continuation of the growth which has already begun is inevitable. During this evolution there are great rewards to be won —by those who are willing to take the opportunities being offered.

(2) 重申主题

再次强调和确定文章开头阐述的中心思想。

例：

Admittedly, science has created atomic bombs and produced pervasive pollution. But it

10

has transformed the lives of millions of people. It has multiplied man's energy, hopes, ambitions and understanding. It has elevated and will continue to elevate man intellectually and spiritually.

（3）预测展望

立足当前，放眼未来。

例：

It is time that the government should speak out against corruption and take strong action to punish whoever takes bribes or embezzles fund. For present official corruption, if permitted to continue, will not only tarnish the government's popularity, but lead to its ultimate downfall.

（4）提出建议

提出解决问题的途径、方法或呼吁人们采取相应的行动。

例：

College athletics plays such a vital role that it deserves close attention and persistent effort. It is suggested that physical training should be regarded as a required course wedged into college curricula, however crowded it may be, and that a fair share of college budget should be devoted to athletic programs. We sincerely hope that this suggestion will be a commitment that all colleges and universities will take up.

（5）提出问题

提出具有发人深省的问题，从而突出中心思想。

例：

Old people may choose to live alone for themselves and even embrace this living pattern. But in the deep part of their hearts, they must feel lonely. They need their children to stay with, to talk with, and take care of them. Why can't young people think of the days when they are getting old?

（6）引用格言

用格言、谚语或习语总括全文中心思想。

例：

Many years ago, a great philosopher Francis Bacon remarked that "Knowledge …is power." This can now be translated into contemporary terms. In our social setting, "Knowledge is change" —and accelerating knowledge-acquisition, fueling the great engine of technology, means accelerating change.

（7）结尾段的核心句型

• From what has been discussed above (Taking into account all these factors / Judging from all evidence offered), we may safely draw (reach / come to / arrive at) the conclusion that …

• All the evidence (analysis) supports (justifies / confirms / warrants / points to) a (n) unshakable (unmistakable / sound / just) conclusion that …

- It is high time that we place (lay / put) great (special / considerable) emphasis on the improvement (development / increase / promotion) of …

- It is high time that we put an end to the deep-seated (unhealthy / undesirable / deplorable) situation (tendency / phenomenon) of …

- We must look (search / call / cry) for an immediate action (method / measure), because the present (current) situation (phenomenon / tendency / state / attitude) of …, if permitted (allowed) to continue (proceed), will surely (certainly) lead to (result in) the end (destruction/ heavy cost) of …

- There is no easy (immediate / effective) solution (approach / answer / remedy) to the problem of … , but … might be useful (helpful / beneficial).

- No easy method (solution / recipe / remedy) can be at hand (found / guaranteed) to solve (resolve / tackle) the problem of …, but the common (general / public) recognition of (realization of / awareness of / commitment to) the necessity (importance / significance) of … might be the first step towards change (on the right way / in the right direction).

- Following these methods (suggestions) may not guarantee the success in (solution to) …, but the pay-off will be worth the effort.

- Obviously (Clearly / No doubt), if we ignore (are blind to) the problem, there is every chance that …

- Unless there is a common realization of (general commitment to) …, it is very likely (the chances are good) that …

- There is little doubt (no denying) that serious (special / adequate / immediate / further) attention must be called (paid / devoted) to the problem of …

- It is necessary (essential/ fundamental) that effective (quick / proper) action (steps / measures / remedies) should be taken to prevent (correct /check / end / fight) the situation (tendency / phenomenon).

- It is hoped (suggested/recommended) that great (continuous /persistent / sustained / corporate) efforts should be made to control (check/ halt / promote) the growth (increase / rise) of …

- It is hoped that great efforts should be directed to (expended on / focused on) finding (developing / improving) …

- It remains to be seen whether …, but the prospect (outlook) is not quite encouraging (that rosy).

- Anyhow, wider (more) education (publicity) should be given to the possible (potential / grave /serious / pernicious) consequences (effects) of …

- To reverse (check / control) the trend (tendency) is not a light task (an easy job), and it requires (demands / involves / entails) a different state of mind towards (attitude towards / outlook on) …

- For these reasons, I strongly recommend that …

- For the reasons given above, I feel that …

4. 段落扩展中的常用词语

（1）总结关系过渡词语

generally speaking, generally, as a general rule, in general, on a larger scale, to take the idea further, to take the above opinion to an extreme, in a sense, in one sense, in a way, to some extent, in my opinion, in my view, as for me, as far as I am concerned, obviously, undoubtedly, in terms of, in conclusion, in short, in brief, in summary, in a word, on the whole, to sum up, to conclude

（2）比较对比关系过渡词语

similarly, likewise, like, too, equally important, the same as, in common, in the same way, on the contrary, on the one hand, on the other hand, otherwise, in sharp contrast, whereas, rather than, conversely, instead, in/by contrast, but, however, yet, nevertheless

（3）列举关系过渡词语

for example, for instance, as an example, as a case in point, such as, namely, that is, like, thus, first, second, third, finally, in the first place, initially, first of all, to begin with, to start with, what is more, furthermore, eventually, besides, in addition (to that), first and foremost, last but not least, next, also, moreover, for one thing, for another

（4）因果关系过渡词语

because (of), as, since, for, owing to, due to, thanks to, on account of, as a result of, result in (from), consequently, for the reason that, as a consequence, consequently, if follows that, accordingly, therefore, hence

（5）让步关系过渡词语

although, even though, after all, in spite of, despite, granted that

（6）强调关系过渡词语

anyway, certainly, surely, obviously, to be sure, especially, particularly, above all, indeed, in fact, even worse, needless to say, most important of all, no doubt

五、考研英语写作程序

由于时间的限制及题型的要求，考生必须遵循一定的写作程序并且合理地分配时间，以便从容地完成较高水平的写作。下面的考研英语写作程序及时间分配，供考生参考并灵活地加以运用。

1. 审题过程（2～3分钟）

所谓"审题"，就是仔细地研究、理解题目，即根据题目所提供的条件和要求，来确定文章的内容、体裁和写法。这一过程直接关系到写作的成败，即是否"切题"。审题应该包含下列四个方面：

（1）审文体

文体是对文章的一种规格要求，不同的文体，在写作上有不同的规格要求。命题作文一般采用议论文文体；规定情景作文通常以描写文、叙述文为主；图表作文通常采用说明文。然

13

而，段首句作文，应视具体内容而定。应用短文写作的文体要求则更加严格。

（2）审内容

了解题目在内容方面的要求决定写什么，这是审题的关键。

（3）审材料

审查考题在选材范围方面的要求，考题对材料有特定的限制，故考生应在题目限制的范围内选取材料。

简言之，选材的一般要点包含：

① 选择真实的材料；

② 选择典型的材料；

③ 选择鲜活的材料；

④ 选择最能展现主题的材料。

（4）审要求

审查考题在格式、字数、时间、内容等诸多方面的具体要求。

总之，如果审题不当，文章跑题；审题不周，文不切题；审题不全，遗漏重点。因此，考生一定要严把审题关。

2. 构思过程（短文写作 5～7 分钟；应用短文写作 2～4 分钟）

一旦确定了主题，就开始构思选材。选材的思路围绕题目、提示、数据、图形和所给的提纲来进行。考生应从自己所熟悉的素材中筛选出最能表达和说明主题的内容，思路要灵活，想象要丰富，同时要有创新，避免落入写作俗套。在此基础上，草拟出作文提纲，提纲要简明扼要，能抓住段落主题。同时，考生对文章段落展开的方法、过渡句和句型等也要有所考虑。

从历年考研英语写作试题来分析，写作题目大多已给出了基本的提纲或相应的要求。在这种情况下，考生可将给出的提纲扩展成相应的主题句，这样便迅速地拟出了一个详细且完整的写作提纲。

拟出带有主题句的具体提纲，才能围绕主题句构思出要写的内容，选出展现主题的最佳素材，形成一条清楚的写作主线，然后根据主线具体地提出和回答 what，who，when，how，why 等一系列考题规定的问题。

3. 下笔创作过程（短文写作 20～25 分钟；应用短文写作 5～10 分钟）

下笔创作过程即段落的展开，考生要用贴切的词与句将自己的所思所想所感一层层地明确表达出来。

考生要注意以下几点：

（1）段落应有段落的主题，并且段落中所涉及的内容都是为文章主题服务的。

（2）写初稿时要一气呵成，尽量不使用自己没有把握的词语或句型。

（3）在下笔创作的过程中可以适当修改提纲，注意不要脱离主题。

（4）注意利用过渡词和过渡句使句子和段落结构严谨连贯，也使内容更易于展开。

4. 检查与修改过程（短文写作 3～5 分钟；应用短文写作 2～3 分钟）

初稿一定存在着某些不妥之处，故需要最后订正。

首先检查内容是否切题，论点是否明确，论据是否充分，结论是否合理，然后检查语法是否正确，语句是否通顺，用词是否贴切，数字是否准确，表达是否恰当，拼写是否正确，标点是否得当等等。

六、考研英语写作常见题型

如果考生想在较短的时间内对考研英语写作有所认识、有所突破，首先应该了解考研英语写作常见题型，并弄懂各种题型的写作技巧，然后进行有针对性的练习，并且研读相关范文。考研英语写作中的常见题型如下：

1. 提纲题型写作

（1）写作要点

① 认真研究所给提纲

考生要注意领会提纲的含义，不要遗漏提纲要点或错误理解提纲的意思。

② 确定各段的主题句

考生应根据所给提纲写出各段的主题句，合格的主题句应具备以下四个要点：

• 意义完整　主题句结构要完整，即结构符合语法规则；意义要完整，即主题句是一个符合逻辑的完整命题。

• 表意清晰　主题句要清晰明确，不使用意思含混的词或句子。

• 内容具体　主题句的内容要明确具体，否则不利于段落的拓展。

• 用词贴切　主题句一定要用词准确，简明达意，使段落的拓展有一个良好的基础。

③ 逐步展开段落

段落写作应围绕自己列好的主题句进行，在写作过程中可稍加调整。

④ 检查与修改

检查考题所给提纲是否准确且完整地被表达于文章之中，如有偏差，应作出相应的修改。

（2）提纲题型写作试题实例

① 写作题目

Title：THE "PROJECT HOPE"

Outline：

i. Present situation

ii. Necessity of the project

iii. My suggestion

② 参考范文：

The "Project Hope"

Education plays a very important role in the modernization of our country. It is well-known that knowledge is power. However, at present, many children in the rural areas drop out of school due to poverty. The case is getting more serious and common in the West of China.

The necessity of the Project Hope can be briefly illustrated as follows. In the first place, the Project Hope itself has aroused the great social concern over the unsatisfactory condition of the childhood education in the rural areas. In the second place, the Project Hope has offered the most needed fund for the drop-outs in the rural areas to return to school. Last but not least important, the Project Hope itself has shown the right way of development to the children in the rural areas—only knowledge can change their fate.

Here are my own suggestions for the "Project Hope". To begin with, relevant laws and regulations must be set up so as to supervise and protect the Project Hope. What's more, a national campaign should be launched to popularize the knowledge of the "Project Hope". Only in this way will more children in the rural areas return to school with the aid of the "Project Hope".

(198 words)

2. 图画题型写作

图画题型写作是较难的题型之一，近两年考研英语写作试题均为图画题型，故考生应该认真对待。面对此类题型，考生应首先确定主题，然后再动笔。

（1）图画题型写作要点

① 详细查看图画。考生应对图画进行全面而细致的研究，尤其注意图画中人或物（人与物）的体貌表情特征和背景，确定人物之间、人物与背景之间的主要关系，以便正确掌握图画所传达的信息。

② 如果图画以系列形式（即两幅以上）出现，考生除了掌握每一幅图画的信息，还应该对图画之间的相应联系有所理解，从而在整体上把握图画所传达的信息。

③ 面对图画题型，考生应该展开合理而丰富的联想，用生动而恰当的言辞抒发自己对图画的所思、所想、所感。

④ 注意图画题型中的文字提示。文字提示非常重要，文字提示通常十分清楚地提供一些写作要点。

⑤ 草拟提纲，合理组织材料。根据图画内容的不同采用不同的段落发展方式。如果画面内容是以描述为主，即按空间方位或时间先后顺序排列，可采用"开头—扩展—结尾"的写作方式。如果画面内容是以解释说明为主，写作时则先给出主题句，再围绕主题句完成各段落的写作，这时可采用"主题句—扩展句—总结句"的写作方式。

⑥ 系统且突出地展开段落。展开段落要根据画面内容进行，同时也要围绕每一段的主题句进行。

⑦ 检查与修改。考生应重点检查图画内容是否准确地被表达出来，题目所给提示是否完整地反映在文章之中。如果存在与画面不相符的内容，或未能完全涵盖题目所给提示，考生应对文章做出相应修订。

（2）图画题型写作试题实例

① 写作题目

Directions:

Study the following set of drawings carefully and write an essay in which you should

a. describe the set of drawings and interpret its meaning, and

b. point out its implications in our life.

You should write about 200 words neatly on ANSWER SHEET 2.

温室花朵经不起风雨

② 参考范文：

The flower in the greenhouse can not withstand the ordeal of wind and storm

As is vividly betrayed by the set of drawings above, a flower is facing two completely different destinies in two different living circumstances. As is shown in the first drawing, the flower is placed in a cozy greenhouse which shelters it from the severe wind and storm. With proper temperature and other good conditions, the flower is growing in full bloom. In contrast, when removed from the greenhouse and exposed to the wind and storm, the flower immediately fades and withers.

The implied meaning subtly conveyed in the drawings should be taken into account more seriously. The weak flower is naturally associated with our young people, to be exact, the only children in our current society; the greenhouse epitomizes our parents' excessive doting care and material supplies that can protect the children from the harsh reality. Once our young people grow up and face challenges from the real competitive world, they are found too spoiled to be strong enough to endure the hardships and difficulties of various sorts.

It is essential for our young people to derive positive implications from the above thought-provoking drawings. On the one hand, we can frequently employ them to enlighten ourselves to be more independent in life. On the other hand, our parents should be sensible enough to offer children more opportunities to cope with their own troubles and problems. Only by undergoing more predicaments can young people possess enough ability needed in the future, and only in this way can they eventually become winners in our competitive world.

(259 words)

3. 表格和图表题型写作

目前，表格和图表题型是考研英语写作中较为常见的题型之一，也是难度较大的一种写作题型，故考生应对此类题型加强练习，熟练掌握。

（1）表格和图表题型写作要点

① 考生应仔细研究题目以及提示信息，看准、看清图表中的数字、线条、阴影等部分的变化趋势和走向，然后根据图表所显示的中心信息确定内容层次以及主题句。

② 考生应该仔细观察分析图表所给出的大量信息，从中选取最重要、最有代表性、最核心的信息，然后根据全文的主旨去组织运用所获取的关键信息。考生应切忌简单地罗列图表所给出的信息。

③ 表格和图表题型写作一般采用一般现在时，但如果图表给出了具体时间参照，考生则应对时态进行相应的调整。

④ 表格和图表题型要求考生使用一些固定句型和表达法，考生应对此融会贯通。

⑤ 表格和图表题型可以细分为表格、曲线图、柱状图和饼状图。除了上述共同要点，考生还应弄懂这四种图在写作方面的各自特点。

• 表格形式要求考生对表格中所给出的大量数字进行比较分析，从中找出其变化规律。

• 曲线图形式要求考生认真观察坐标系所显示的数据信息，并且密切注意交会在坐标横轴和纵轴上的数字及单位。

• 柱状图形式要求考生通过宽度相等的柱形的高度或长度差别来判断事物的动态发展趋势，故考生应密切关注坐标线上的刻度单位及图表旁边的提示说明与文字。

• 饼状图形式旨在要求考生准确理解并阐述一个被分割成大小不等切片的饼状图所传达的信息。考生应清楚掌握部分与整体、部分与部分之间的相互关系，这种关系通常是以百分比的数字形式给出的。

⑥ 列出各段的主题句。考生可以根据所给提纲或已知信息列出每段的主题句，为全文的展开铺平道路。

⑦ 严格围绕主题句展开段落。

⑧ 检查与修改。表格与图表写作的检查与修改应着重检查文章中所列举的信息是否与图表所显示的信息一致。

（2）表格和图表题型的核心句型

句型1：

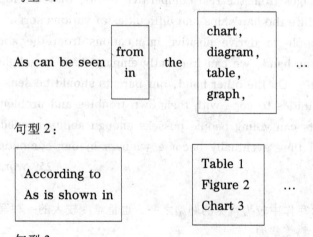

句型2：

句型3：

18

It can be seen from the | chart / diagram / table / graph / figures / statistics | that ...

句型 4：

From the | table / figures / data / results / information | it | can / may | be | seen / concluded / shown / estimated / calculated / inferred | that ...

句型 5：

During the period 1998—2009
From 1998 to 2008
Since 2007
For a hundred years, from 1910 to 2010, ...

句型 6：

There | is / was / has been | a | slight / small / slow / gradual / steady / large / dramatic / sharp / rapid / sudden | rise / increase / fluctuation / decrease / decline / reduction / fall / drop | in | prices. / population. / production. / personal income. / demand. / water supply.

句型 7：

The first thing we have
First of all, I should like | to consider ...

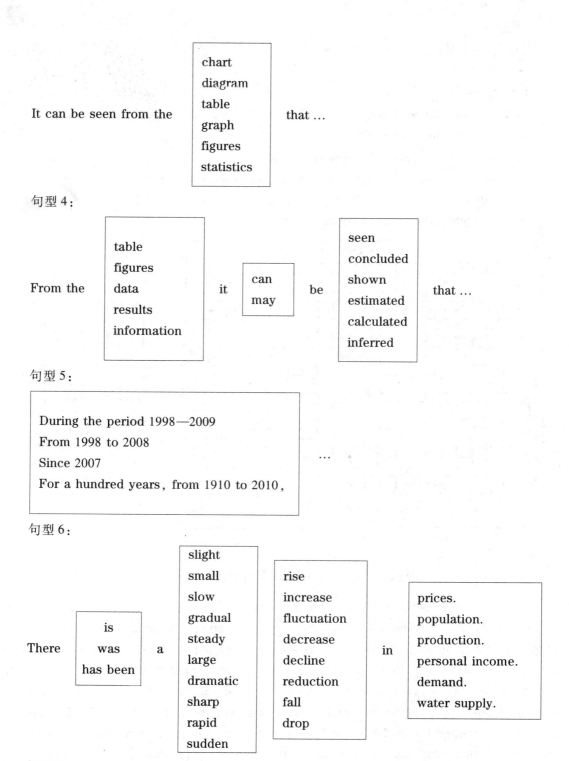

19

（3）表格和图表题型写作试题实例

① 写作题目

Directions：

A. Study the following graphs carefully and write an essay in about 200 words.

B. Your essay must be written neatly on ANSWER SHEET 2.

C. Your essay should cover these three points:

a. effect of the country's growing human population on its wildlife；

b. possible reason for the effect；

c. your suggestion for the wildlife protection.

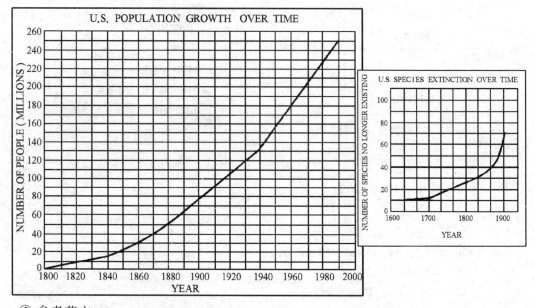

② 参考范文：

Population Growth and Species Extinction

As is accurately betrayed by the two graphs above, during the period of time from 1800 to 1990, with the explosive growth of the U. S. population, the number of extinct species shot up, amounting to 70 in 1900. It is apparent that the population explosion resulted in the sharp decline of the wildlife of the country. What brought about this fact?

There are, I do deem, two potential reasons for the fact. To begin with, the ever-increasing population needs more land to grow crops and more space to live in. Consequently, there is less and less niche in the U. S. for wildlife. Moreover, a number of newly built factories which produce daily necessities for the explosive population keep discharging harmful gases and liquids, which seriously pollute the environment. The environmental pollution has disturbed the ecological balance, contributing to the extinction of some wildlife.

In my view, three strong measures should be taken to solve the problem. In the first place, the birth rate in the U. S. must be put under control because the rapidly growing population leads to serious environmental crisis. In the second place, the U. S. government is supposed to create as many nature reserves as possible where all the native species of wild animals can be kept from being hunted and all the native species of plants can grow vigorously. Last but not least important, it is urgent for the authorities to set up laws to reward those who do much to protect wildlife. (246 words)

4. 情景题型写作

（1）情景题型写作要点

情景题型写作没有具体题目，仅仅规定一定的情景，这是一种指导性较强的写作题型，考生千万不要脱离情景，而应严格依照题目所规定的情景构思短文。特别注意以下几点：

① 情景式写作要求考生在题目规定的情景内展开构思，组织内容。

② 仔细审题。考生应明确题目所提供的情景，是论证还是说明，是叙事还是写景。

③ 确定段落与主题句。各段的主题句使文章有条有理，同时也使考生对自己所要表达的内容有更具体的把握。

④ 平稳地展开段落。主题句一经确定，考生便可以围绕主题句，展开段落，完成全文的写作。段的展开应该建立在段落情景基础之上，每段的重点都应集中于描述情景规定内容。

⑤ 考生的每一词每一句应紧扣情景，突出重点，前后连贯，表达清楚，符合逻辑。

⑥ 明确题型种类。情景写作可根据内容写成不同文体，如记叙文、论说文、书信报告等，故考生应该注意灵活运用相应文体的写作方法与技巧。

⑦ 认真检查与修改。考生应重点检查作文是否完全准确地包含了情景所要求的各方面内容，是否有与情景相悖或不相关的内容。

（2）情景题型写作实例

① 考试题目：

Some people hold onto the idea that money and property offer more opportunities for success in our society; others think that education provide more opportunities for success in our society. Present your perspective on the issue, using relevant reasons and/or examples to support your views.

② 参考范文：

Which factor offers more opportunities for success in our society: education or money and property? In my view, education has replaced money and property as the main provider of such opportunities today. I base my view on two reasons. First, education—particularly higher education—used to be amiable only to the wealthy but now is accessible to almost anyone. Second, because of the civil-rights movement and resulting laws, businesses are now required to hire on the basis of merit rather than the kinds of personal relations traditionally common among the wealthy.

Education always plays a key role in determining one's opportunities for success. But in the past, good post-secondary education was available mainly to the privileged classes. Because money and property largely determined one's access to higher education, money and property really were the critical factors in opening doors to success. However, higher education is more egalitarian today. Given our vast numbers of state universities and financial-aid programs, virtually anyone who meets entrance requirements for college can obtain an excellent college education and open up windows of opportunity in life.

Another reason those opportunities will be open to educated young people from middle-class and poorer background is that hiring is more merit-oriented today than ever before. In principle, at least, our country has always been a society where all people are equal; yet in the past, children of the wealthy and well-connected could expect to obtain higher-status jobs and to receive better pay. But the laws and programs resulting from our civil-rights struggles have produced a modern business climate in which jobs are available on an equal-opportunity basis, and in which candidates have a legal right to be judged on the merit of their educational background and experience.

In conclusion, education is probably the main factor in opening doors to success for young people in our society. The fact that education has supplanted money and property in this role is attributable to a more egalitarian system of higher education, as well as to more merit-based hiring practices that generally value individual education over family fortune or relation. (347 words)

5. 摘要题型写作

摘要题型写作是难度非常大的一种写作形式。随着考生英语水平的不断提高,这种题型应引起考生的普遍重视。

(1) 摘要题型写作要点:

① 动笔之前,考生一定要认真仔细地阅读所给原文,弄懂原文大意,掌握原文要点。

② 摘要的长度一般是原文的四分之一或五分之一,考试时应遵守规定的字数限制。

③ 在做摘要时考生切忌照搬原文。

④ 摘要应与原文的观点保持一致,并且仍按原文的逻辑顺序排列。

⑤ 重点反映主要观点,删除细节。

⑥ 简化从句,用简短的语句代替冗长的语句。

⑦ 检查与修改时,考生应重点检查是否遗漏了原文的要点或包含了细节。

(2) 摘要题型写作实例

① 试题题目

Directions:

Study the following essay carefully and write a summary in about 80 words.

We continue to share with our remotest ancestors the most tangled and evasive attitudes about death, despite the great distance we have come in understanding some of the profound aspects of biology. We have as much distaste for talking about personal death as for thinking about it; it is an indelicacy, like talking in mixed company about venereal disease or abortion in the old days. Death on a grand scale does not bother us in the same special way: we can sit around a dinner table and discuss war, involving 60 billion volatilized human deaths, as though we were talking about bad weather; we can watch abrupt bloody death every day, in color, on films and television, without blinking back a tear. It is when the numbers of dead are very small, and very close, that we begin to think in scurrying circles. At the very center of the problem is the naked cold deadness of one's own self, the only reality in nature of which we can have absolute certainty, and it is unmentionable, unthinkable. We may be even less willing to face the issue at first hand than our predecessors because of a secret new hope that maybe it will go away. We like to think, hiding the thought, that with all the marvelous ways in which we seem now to lead nature around by the nose, perhaps we can avoid the central problem if we just become, next year, say, a bit smarter.　　(246 words)

② 原文要点：

i. continue to have the most confused ideas of death like predecessors

ii. avoid talking about death

iii. talk about death when millions of people die

iv. become confused and anxious when each time the dead people are very few and the death rates are almost equal

v. people's fearfulness

vi. seem to control nature

vii. avoid death

③ 参考摘要：

People dislike talking about death because they just like their predecessors still have the vaguest ideas of the issue. They talk about death only when millions upon millions of people are killed in war. When they find only very few people die each time and the death rates are almost equal, they become very anxious, thinking that next time they themselves will meet their doom. Therefore, they fear very much. However, they have a hope that when they control nature, they can avoid death.　(84 words)

6. 书信题型写作

书信题型写作是常见的功能性写作形式，考生应该对书信写作的具体细节有整体的把握。

（1）书信写作要点

① 日期

写信人应将写信日期（年、月、日）放在书信正文的右上角，如 February 3rd, 2011。

② 称呼

称呼是写信人对收信人的称谓，称呼可以根据收信人的性别、职务、婚姻状况、姓名等个人信息来写，如：Mr. Williams, Mrs. Bush, Professor Li, Dr. Smith, Dear Mum and Dad。如果写信人不清楚收信人的具体姓名、职务等情况，可以写：Dear Sir or Madam

③ 正文

正文是书信的主要部分，在称呼下方隔一或两行处开始。考生写正文时，要分层次进行。书信正文通常由引言、展开段和结尾三个层次组成。

• 引言　引言表明写信人的写信目的和写信背景，一般仅限于一段，一两句话即可。

- 展开段　展开段内容应翔实、具体。可以分为若干段来写，每一段围绕一个主题进行展开。
- 结尾　结尾部分通常比引言部分短，使用一两句话表达一下希望或祝愿。

④ 结束语

结束语是写信人对收信人的谦称，写在正文下面二至三行处。公务等较正式的信件多采用 Yours sincerely, Sincerely yours, Yours faithfully, Yours truly 等；私人信件，多采用 Yours, With love, Yours affectionately 等。

⑤ 签名

签名应写在结束语的下面。

（2）书信题型写作实例

① 试题题目：

Directions：

A. Write a job application letter of about 100 words

B. Your letter should cover these three points：

a. apply for the position of production coordinator

b. describe your education background

c. state your relevant working experience

② 参考范文：

Jan. 15, 2011

Dear Sir or Madam,

I am responding to your ad in the Jan. 8th 2011, issue of the Sunday *Talent Journal* for the position of production coordinator. I feel that my background in electronics and manufacturing will fit in well.

I will graduate from the Beijing Science & Technology University in August with a Bachelor of Science degree in Manufacturing Engineering. I have had extensive training on computers while at school.

As shown in my resume, I have also repaired and installed fire alarm, security, and patient-signal systems when I worked at Johnson Controls. Most of the time I faced construction deadlines so I know what it is like to work under pressure.

I am looking forward to hearing from you. Would you please call me to set up an interview? I can be reached at my resume address or by phoning (010) 82073660 after 4 p. m.

Sincerely,

Li Ming

(147 words)

以上是针对考研英语写作与对策进行的概述，这是考研写作的理论。考生在掌握理论的基础之上，应该加强练习。俗话说："熟读唐诗三百首，不会做诗也会吟"。具体地讲，考生应该多接触一些写作题目，多精研一些范文，从中找出写作的规律和技巧。另外，熟背一定数量的范文对考生是十分重要的。正是为了这一点，我们编写了本书，希望大家能从本书的学习中寻找出突破考研写作的方法，为取得考研高分奠定坚实的基础。

第二部分 考研英语短文写作
备考试题（1~50篇）

考研英语短文写作备考试题　第1篇

写作题目与要求

Study the following drawing carefully and write an essay in which you should
1）describe the drawing briefly,
2）explain the intended purpose of the painter, and then
3）give your comments.
You should write about 160~200 words neatly on ANSWER SHEET 2. （20 points）

具体写作思路

1. 第一段的描述要涉及文明和技巧这两个要点。
2. 第二段着重讨论体育精神的重要性和必要性。
3. 第三段要提出两条具体的改进措施：立法和教育。

参考范文

　　As is vividly revealed in the drawing above, a football player is competing with both his professional skills and sports spirit. The meaning conveyed in the drawing is of importance to the development of the sports games.

　　The aim of the painter of the drawing can be briefed as follows. To begin with, it is urgent for some players to cultivate necessary sports spirit. At present, some players are so money-oriented that they often sacrifice sports spirit to gain their personal interests. For instance, some players take drugs prohibited by IOC while others are involved in notorious sports <u>gambling</u>. When players lose their sports spirit, the value of sports is gone. What's more, players with both super professional skills and excellent sports spirit are players badly needed at the moment. <u>Owing to</u> the more <u>frequent</u> international exchange, we not only need <u>athletes</u> with wonderful skills to display the rapid growth of Chinese sports but also want athletes with first-class sports spirit to demonstrate our national <u>image</u> and win the world over. On the whole, to keep the <u>sustainable</u> development of sports and to establish our international image depend upon both the professional skills and sports spirit.

In my view, effective measures should be taken to <u>reverse</u> the grim <u>status</u>. First of all, laws and regulations must be set up to <u>curb</u> the players' misconduct. In addition, an education campaign should be <u>launched</u> to popularize sports spirit among athletes, especially the young. Only in these ways can we really enjoy sports games and win the respect of the world.

(258 words)

一句话点评

在第二段中有关国家形象的论点有深度，这是高分短文写作的必备条件之一。

全文翻译

如同上面图画所生动显示的一样，一名足球运动员正在用他的专业技能和体育精神进行比赛。这幅画所传达的含义对于体育运动的发展是重要的。

本图作者的目的可简述如下。首先，培养一些球员必要的体育精神是迫切的。目前，一些球员太向"钱"看，以至于他们通常牺牲体育精神来获得个人利益。例如，一些球员服用国际奥委会所禁止的药物，同时另外一些球员卷入臭名昭著的体育赌博。当球员丧失体育精神时，体育的价值也消失了。此外，既具有超级专业技巧又具有出色体育精神的球员是现在所急需的球员。由于更加频繁的国际交流，我们不仅需要具有出色技巧的运动员来展示中国体育运动的迅速发展，还需要具有一流体育精神的运动员来展现我们的民族形象并且赢得世界。总之，保持体育的可持续发展并且确立我们的国际形象，取决于专业技巧和体育精神。

我认为，应该采取有效的措施来扭转目前严峻的状况。首先一定要确立法规来制止球员的不良行为。此外，应该在运动员中开展一场教育运动，尤其在年轻运动员中，普及体育精神。只有以这些方法，我们才能真正享受体育运动并且赢得世界的尊重。

重点写作词语点睛

professional a. 专业的；职业的	involve v. 卷入；涉及
as follows 如下	notorious a. 臭名昭著的
cultivate v. 培养	gambling n. 赌博
money-oriented 向钱看的	owing to 由于
sacrifice v. 牺牲	frequent a. 频繁的
drug n. 毒品	athlete n. 运动员
prohibit v. 禁止	image n. 形象

sustainable　*a.* 可持续的　　　　curb　*v.* 抑制
reverse　*v.* 扭转　　　　　　　launch　*v.* 开展
status　*n.* 状况

考研英语短文写作备考试题　　第 2 篇

写作题目与要求

Study the following drawing carefully and write an essay in which you should

1）describe the drawing briefly,

2）explain its intended meaning, and then

3）give your comments.

You should write about 160 ~ 200 words neatly on ANSWER SHEET 2. （20 points）

——大学生救人

摘自　曹一/绘画

具体写作思路

1. 第一段的描述要表达人们对 90 后大学生壮举的肯定。

2. 第二段围绕舍己救人是大学生的本能进行阐述和分析。

3. 第三段通过谈论生命可以升华来发表自己的看法。

参考范文

As is vividly demonstrated in the drawing above, three university students from Yangtze University, who were born in the 1990s, were away from us. People are deeply moved by their heroic <u>deeds</u> and <u>speak highly of</u> them. What is conveyed in the drawing makes us reflect on our own daily conducts and behavior.

The implication of the drawing can be interpreted as follows. To begin with, the three heroes' sacrifice is precious because it <u>defies</u> the current mindless trend of self-centeredness. When the students jumped into the cold water, they did not think about how the world would judge them. They did not have enough time to think about the <u>potential</u> dangers either. They acted only out of <u>instinct</u>, the human instinct of saving another human. What's more, this instinct is <u>nurtured</u> by our parents and teachers. It is the result of the culture <u>rooted</u> in our <u>soil</u>. It is reassuring to know that our tradition of valuing and admiring a sacrifice has <u>passed on</u> to the present generation. It is also reassuring to see that the <u>concept</u> of "protecting one's own life is far more important than fighting a crime or saving another life" is not the <u>motto</u> of all our youths. We should be <u>grateful</u>, too, to the three students for carrying forward the spirit of <u>humanity</u> and the nation.

In my view, the debate over worthy or unworthy of their action will never come to a conclusion. The only thing certain is the <u>principle</u> that life is the highest good. The value of one's life can also be <u>escalated</u> to higher <u>moral</u> value by <u>cherishing</u> others' lives. What we should do is to stop quarrelling and <u>care for</u> the heroes' <u>families</u>.　　　　　　　　(283 words)

一句话点评

在第二段中有关舍己救人与民族精神的联系有思想深度，这是高分短文写作所不可缺少的内容。

全文翻译

如上面的图画所生动地展示，三位长江大学的 90 后大学生离开了我们。人们被他们的英雄行为所深深地感动并且赞扬他们的行为。本图所传递的内容使我们反省我们自己的日常行为和举止。

本图的含义可以解释如下。首先，三位英雄的牺牲是宝贵的，因为他们的牺牲挑战了目前以自我为中心的发展趋势。当他们跳入冰冷的江水时，他们没有想过这个世界会如何评价他们。他们也没有足够的时间去考虑可能的危险。他们的行为仅仅是出于本能，挽救他人的人类本能。此外这种本能是家长和老师所培育的。这种本能是扎根于我们民族土壤的文化结果。令人感到欣慰的是，我们知道了尊重和赞赏牺牲的传统已经传递到目前的一代人身上。另外感到欣慰的是，我们认识到保护自己的生命比与犯罪作斗争或者挽救他人的生命更重要这一想法并不是所有年轻人的座右铭。我们还应该感谢这三位大学生，因为他们发扬光大了人类和民族的精神。

我认为有关他们的行为值得或者不值得的争论永远也不会有定论。但是，可以肯定的是生命高于一切的原则。通过爱惜别人的生命，一个人的生命价值可以被提升到更高的道德价值。我们应该做的是停止争论，转而去关爱英雄的家人。

重点写作词语点睛

deed　　*n.* 行为	potential　　*a.* 潜在的
speak highly of　肯定	instinct　　*n.* 本能
defy　*v.* 挑战	nurture　*v.* 培养

root *v.* 扎根	principle *n.* 原则
soil *n.* 土壤	escalate *v.* 上升；升级
pass on 传递	moral *a.* 道德的
concept *n.* 概念	cherish *v.* 珍惜
motto *n.* 座右铭	care for 关爱
grateful *a.* 感激的；感谢的	family *n.* 家人
humanity *n.* 人性；人类	

考研英语短文写作备考试题　　第3篇

写作题目与要求

Study the following drawing carefully and write an essay in which you should

1）describe the drawing briefly，

2）explain its intended meaning，and then

3）give your comments.

You should write about 160～200 words neatly on ANSWER SHEET 2.（20 points）

——斑马线上的杀手

具体写作思路

1. 第一段的描述要突出刻画酒后驾车司机对行人的无礼。
2. 第二段围绕个人行为和道德价值观这两点进行阐述。
3. 第三段从法律和教育这两点提出应对措施。

参考范文

　　As is vividly depicted in the drawing above，a drink-driver is scolding a pedestrian who is crossing a street at zebra crossing. What is revealed in the drawing is not uncommon in our routine life and the phenomenon is most thought-provoking to each responsible citizen of our society.

The intention of its painter can be interpreted in terms of personal manners and moral values. To begin with, good manners should be advocated in our daily life. Some people are quite selffish and only care about their own interests. Sometimes, they even violate the social rules and regulations in pursuit of their own convenience and benefits. As a consequence, our society would be filled with selfishness and hatred. What's more, traditional moral values should be upheld. There is no doubt that over the past decades our material life has been considerably improved. However, such traditional moral values as mutual help, understanding, and courtesy are ignored. As a result, we are alien to each other and building a harmonious society is beyond our reach. In short, the drawing does awaken us to a grim reality.

As far as I am concerned, strict measures must be immediately taken so as to reverse the current situation. On the one hand, a nationwide campaign should be launched to educate people about the significance of good manners and moral values. On the other hand, relevant laws and regulations must be established and strictly implemented. Only in these ways can we live in a harmonious society and enjoy the benefits of modern civilization.

(254 words)

一句话点评

在第二段中有关传统道德价值观的论述有思想深度，这是高分短文写作所需要的内容。

全文翻译

如同上面的图画所生动地描绘，一名酒后驾车者正在大骂一位在人行横道上穿越马路的行人。本图所显示的内容在我们生活中是常见的，并且这种现象对于每一个有责任的公民而言都是非常发人深省的。

本图画作者的目的可以从个人行为和道德价值观这两个方面加以解释。首先，在我们的日常生活中应该倡导良好的行为。一些人十分自私并且仅仅关心他们的个人利益。有时候他们在追求自我便利和好处的过程中甚至破坏社会规章制度。其结果，我们的社会会充满自私和仇恨。此外，传统的道德价值应该得到坚持和维护。毫无疑问，在过去的几十年里我们的物质生活已经大大地改善。然而，传统的道德价值观，例如互助、理解以及礼貌，却被忽略了。其结果，我们彼此非常陌生，并且构建和谐社会也遥不可及。总之，这幅图画的确让我们清醒地认识到了一个无情的现实。

我认为，应该采取严格的措施以便扭转目前的局势。一方面，应该开展一场全国范围的运动，以便就良好行为和道德价值观的重要性对人们进行教育。另一方面，相关法律和制度应该得到确立并且严格地执行。只有以这两种方式我们才能生活在一个和谐的社会中，并且享受现代文明的益处。

重点写作词语点睛

scold v. 骂	routine a. 日常的
pedestrian n. 行人	thought-provoking 发人深省的

intention *n.* 意图	There is no doubt that... 毫无疑问
in terms of 从…方面而言	material *n.* 物质
advocate *v.* 提倡	mutual *a.* 相互的
care about 关心	courtesy *n.* 礼貌
interest *n.* 利益	ignore *v.* 忽略；忽视
violate *v.* 违反	harmonious *a.* 和谐的
in pursuit of 追求	grim *a.* 无情的
as a consequence 其结果	campaign *n.* 运动
hatred *n.* 恨	implement *v.* 执行
uphold *v.* 坚持	civilization *n.* 文明

考研英语短文写作备考试题　　第 4 篇

写作题目与要求

Study the following drawing carefully and write an essay in which you should

1）describe the drawing briefly，

2）explain the intended purpose of the painter，and then

3）give your comments.

You should write about 160~200 words neatly on ANSWER SHEET 2.（20 points）

——吉祥歌舞

具体写作思路

1. 第一段的描述要反映各民族的人民在祖国怀抱中的快乐。

2. 第二段要从我国的多民族特点和民族团结的意义这两方面进行阐述。

3. 第三段要结合新疆等地的实际情况加以表述。

参考范文

As is vividly demonstrated in the drawing above，people of different ethnic groups in

China are singing and dancing merrily in front of the rostrum of Tian'anmen. Singing and dancing performances reflect the best wishes for our motherland. What is conveyed in the drawing is most meaningful and far-reaching.

The aim of the painter can be interpreted as follows. First of all, China is a ethnic community in which all its ethnic groups are interdependent. The unified multiethnic country is spread over a vast territory and is home to a splendid culture. The foundation for the country has been laid by all its ethnic groups, and forms the basis of its national solidarity. What's more, the country's ethnic groups have strengthened their social and emotional bonds over a long period. As our history of thousands of years shows, unity and stability bring development and prosperity, and benefit all the people, while secessionism and unrest result in stagnancy and distress, and damage the interest of every person. Therefore, national unity and social stability is where the highest national interests of Chinese nation lie.

In my view, three decades of reform and opening up have helped many ethnic minority areas to turn into booming economies, and Xinjiang is no exception. Chinese people should cherish their national unity, not violate it. They should preserve the hopeful development trend, not reverse it. And they should cash in on the historic opportunity, not let it slip by. We urge all members of our society to help safeguard social order, national unity and the interest of the nation.

(259 words)

一句话点评

在第二段中有关民族团结与社会安定和繁荣之间关系的论述具有思想深度，这是高分短文写作不可缺少的内容。

全文翻译

如同上面的图画所生动地显示，中国不同民族的人们在天安门城楼前高兴地唱歌跳舞。他们的歌舞反映了对祖国的良好祝愿。本幅图画所传递的内容非常耐人寻味并且意义深远。

本幅图画作者的目的可以解释如下。首先，中国是一个民族集体。在这个集体中，所有的民族群体相互依赖。这个团结的多民族国家分布在辽阔的疆土上并且孕育了灿烂的文化。国家的基础是由各民族群体创造的，并且形成了国家团结的根基。此外，长期以来国家的民族群体加强了他们的社会和情感联系。正如几千年的历史所示，团结和稳定带来了发展和繁荣，并且使所有人获益。背离祖国和动乱产生停滞和痛苦，并且损害每个人的利益。因此，民族团结和社会稳定是中华民族最高利益之所在。

我认为改革开放的 30 年帮助许多少数民族地区转变成为繁荣经济地区，新疆也不例外。中国人应该珍惜民族团结而不是破坏它。中国人应该保护充满希望的发展趋势，而不是破坏这一趋势。中国人应该抓住历史的机遇而不是让机会溜掉。我们要求社会的所有成员帮助维护社会秩序、民族团结和国家利益。

重点写作词语点睛

ethnic *a.* 民族的

interdependent *a.* 相互依赖的

unified *a.* 团结的

multiethnic *a.* 多民族的

territory *n.* 领土

splendid *a.* 灿烂的

unity *n.* 团结

bond *n.* 结合；联合

stability *n.* 稳定

prosperity *n.* 繁荣

benefit *v.* 有益于

secessionism *n.* 脱离主义

unrest *n.* 动乱

stagnancy *n.* 停滞

distress *n.* 痛苦

interest *n.* 利益

lie *v.* 存在，在（于）

minority *n.* 少数民族

booming *a.* 繁荣的，发展的

exception *n.* 例外

cherish *v.* 珍惜

preserve *v.* 保护

cash in on 依靠

slip by 悄然逝去

safeguard *v.* 维护，捍卫

order *n.* 秩序

考研英语短文写作备考试题   第 5 篇

写作题目与要求

Study the following drawing carefully and write an essay in which you should

1）describe the drawing briefly,

2）explain its intended meaning, and then

3）give your comments.

You should write about 160 ~ 200 words neatly on ANSWER SHEET 2.（20 points）

社会责任　个人利益

明星 代言

——明星代言

具体写作思路

1. 第一段的描述要涉及社会责任和个人利益这两个要点。
2. 第二段围绕明星的社会责任以及诚信的建设这两点展开分析和论述。
3. 第三段从法律和教育的角度去发表个人的观点。

参考范文

As is vividly demonstrated in the drawing above, a woman star is making advertising for products of a brand. The star focuses on personal benefits while turning a blind eye on social responsibilities. What the drawing intends to convey is most meaningful and thought-provoking.

The intended meaning of the drawing can be interpreted with respect to the stars' social responsibility and the establishment of credibility. On the one hand, some stars and celebrities lack basic social responsibilities. Stars and celebrities should play a positive role in our daily life since they are considered as social models. However, some stars are so money-oriented that they conduct irresponsible deeds, which cause negative effects in our society. On the other hand, the establishment of credibility needs to be put on the top of our agenda. The misconducts of some stars and celebrities indicate that they are losing their basic sense of credibility. The misleading remarks which are made by some stars and celebrities not only endanger our physical body but also our mind and soul. A world of cheating and money-desire is doomed to perish. In one word, stars should mind their social roles and our credibility needs to be minded.

In my view, some urgent measures should be taken so as to reverse the current grim situation. To begin with, education campaign should be launched to guide stars and celebrities to behave well. In addition, basic laws and regulations should be set up to get rid of dishonest words and deeds. Only in these ways can we create a harmonious living environment.

(262 words)

一句话点评

在第二段中对于明星不负责任的行为所产生的不良后果的论述十分深刻，这是高分短文写作所应具备的思想深度。

全文翻译

如同上面的图画所生动地显示，一位女明星正在为一个品牌的产品做广告。该明星关注个人利益，而对社会责任却视而不见。本图所要传达的内容是非常耐人寻味并且发人深省的。

图画的含义可以从明星责任与诚信的建设这两个方面来解释。一方面，一些明星和名人缺乏社会责任感。明星和名人应该在日常生活中起积极的作用，因为他们被视为社会的榜样。然而，一些明星太向钱看了，以至于他们做出不负责的行为，这在社会中造成了负面影响。另一方面，诚信的建立需要放在我们的议事日程。一些明星和名人的不当行为显示：他们正在丧失他

35

们基本的诚信感。明星说的误导性言语不仅危害我们的身体，而且伤害我们的心灵。一个充满欺骗和钱欲的世界注定灭亡。总之，明星应该注意他们的社会角色。我们需要加强我们的诚信。

我认为：应该采取一些迫切的措施以扭转目前严峻的形势。首先，应该开展一场教育运动来引导明星和名人端正行为。另外，应该制定法规以消除不诚实的言行。只有以这些方式，我们才能创造一个和谐的生活环境。

重点写作词语点睛

advertising	*n.* 广告	model	*n.* 榜样
brand	*n.* 品牌	conduct	*v.* 从事，做
focus on	聚焦	negative	*a.* 消极的
responsibility	*n.* 责任	agenda	*n.* 议事日程
with respect to	就…而言	misleading	*a.* 误导人的
credibility	*n.* 诚信	doom	*v.* 注定
celebrity	*n.* 名人	perish	*v.* 消亡
positive	*a.* 积极的	launch	*v.* 开展

考研英语短文写作备考试题　第6篇

写作题目与要求

Study the following drawing carefully and write an essay in which you should

1）describe the drawing briefly,

2）explain the intended purpose of the painter, and then

3）give your comments.

You should write about 160～200 words neatly on ANSWER SHEET 2. （20 points）

——农民工

具体写作思路

1. 第一段的描述要反映农民工的劳动和生活环境之间的差异。
2. 第二段围绕农民工对社会的具体贡献展开阐述。
3. 第三段从为农民工做些什么这一角度发表自己的观点。

参考范文

As is realistically revealed in the drawings above, a <u>migrant worker</u> is working hard at apartment construction while living in a <u>shabby</u> house. Such facts are just around us. Therefore, what is conveyed in the drawings above is most thought-provoking and should arouse the <u>concern</u> of our society.

The aim of the painter can be interpreted as follows. To begin with, none of our <u>achievements</u> in the past three decades would have been possible without these migrant workers. They build new apartments for innumerable Chinese. They construct roads, railways, bridges and tunnels. They <u>give shape to</u> engineering <u>marvels</u> such as the Qinghai-Tibet Railway, the Three Gorges Dam, Beijing's Bird's Nest, Shanghai's Lujiazui skyline, and the 36-km-long bridge across the Hangzhou Bay. What's more, they are the <u>backbone</u> of the country's <u>competitive</u> export industry as an estimated 80 million of them work long hours for low wages in factories and on <u>assembly lines</u>. These people are essential for the <u>smooth</u> operation of our cities and our families, as they wait in restaurants, <u>deliver</u> milk, clean our streets and tidy our homes.

In my view, our <u>appreciation</u> should definitely go beyond words. Each of us should ask what we can do for migrant workers. Would you smile at them and say thank you the next time you see them? Would you <u>embrace</u> them as our brothers and sisters and an equal member of our society? And would you help <u>secure</u> their rights, such as their rights to labor protection and their children's rights to equal education? There are a million of things we can do for migrant workers. It would be no <u>hype</u> to have a Migrant Workers Day in the year, in order to <u>honor</u> their contribution and remind us what we should do for these heroes.

(298 words)

一句话点评

在第二段中有关农民工对社会具体贡献的阐述感人至深，这是高分短文写作的法宝。

全文翻译

如同上面图画所真实地展现，一位农民工正在努力工作盖公寓楼，同时他自己却住在破旧的房子里。这样的现象就在我们的身边。因此，图画中所传递的内容是非常发人深省的，并且应该唤起社会的关注。

图画作者的目的可以解释如下。首先，没有这些农民工，在过去的三十年里所取得的任何成就都是不可能实现的。他们为无数的中国人盖建新的楼房。他们建设公路、铁路、桥梁和隧道。他们塑造了工程学上的奇迹，例如青藏铁路、三峡大坝、北京鸟巢、上海陆家嘴摩天大厦以及 36 公里长的跨杭州湾大桥。此外，他们是中国具有竞争力的出口行业的支柱，因为大约八千万农民工在工厂和装配线上超时地工作。这些农民工对于城市和家庭的正常运转也是重要的，因为他们在饭店当服务员、送牛奶、清理街道并且整理我们的家务。

我认为，我们的感激之情肯定超越了语言所能表达的范围。我们每一个人应该问一问：我们能为农民工做些什么。当你下次遇到农民工的时候，你会对他们微笑并且说感谢你们吗？你会把他们当作你的兄弟姐妹和我们社会的平等成员吗？你会帮助他们保证他们的权力，例如劳动保护的权力和其子女接受同等教育的权力吗？我们有许多能为农民工去做的事情。一年中设立一个农民工日，以便肯定他们的贡献并且提醒我们能为这些英雄做些什么，这绝不是说得天花乱坠的广告。

重点写作词语点睛

migrant worker　农民工	assembly line　装配线
shabby　*a.* 破旧的，失修的	smooth　*a.* 顺利的
concern　*n.* 关注	deliver　*v.* 送
achievement　*n.* 成就	appreciation　*n.* 感谢，感激
give shape to　塑造	embrace　*v.* 接受
marvel　*n.* 奇迹	secure　*v.* 保证
backbone　*n.* 支柱	hype　*n.* 天花乱坠的广告
competitive　*a.* 有竞争力的	honor　*v.* 尊重

考研英语短文写作备考试题　　第7篇

写作题目与要求

Study the following drawing carefully and write an essay in which you should

1）describe the drawing briefly,

2）explain its intended meaning, and then

3）give your comments.

You should write about 160 ~ 200 words neatly on ANSWER SHEET 2. （20 points）

——全球变暖
摘自《中国日报》

具体写作思路

1. 第一段的描述要突出反映全球变暖这一核心问题。
2. 第二段围绕目前的相关状况和人类应有的相关认识加以阐述。
3. 第三段要从呼吁大家行动起来这一角度发表自己的见解。

参考范文

As is realistically revealed in the drawing above, our planet is sweating all over and can hardly move forward due to global warming-up effect. What is conveyed in the drawing is most thought-provoking and should arouse the concern of the international community.

The implication of the drawing can be interpreted as follows. To begin with, as the planet warms, rainfall patterns shift, and extreme events such as droughts, floods, and forest fires become more frequent. Millions in densely populated coastal areas and in island nations will lose their homes as the sea level rises. In Africa, Asia, and elsewhere, poor people face prospects of tragic crop failures, reduced agricultural productivity, and increasing hunger, malnutrition, and disease. Climate change is one of the most complex challenges of our young century. What's more, such a transformation requires us to act now and act together. We must act now, because what we do today determines both the climate of tomorrow and the choices that shape our future. We must act together, because climate change is a crisis of the commons. Climate change cannot be solved without countries cooperating on a global scale. We need to protect human life and ecological resources.

In my view, much more is needed. We need action on climate issues before it is too late. If we act now and act together, there are real opportunities to shape our climate future for a safe and sustainable globalization. China will cut carbon dioxide emissions per unit of

GDP by 40 to 45 percent by 2020, taking 2005 as the base year. We do not need to wait for a low-carbon future. It starts now.

(274 words)

一句话点评

在第二段中有关目前人类所处境地的描述简明具体,这是高分短文写作所要求的写作方式。

全文翻译

如同上图所真实地展现,由于全球变暖效应,我们的星球大汗淋漓并且几乎不能向前行走。图画所传递的内容是非常发人深省的,并且应该唤起国际社会的关注。

本幅图画的含义可以解释如下。首先,由于我们的星球变暖,降雨方式发生了变化,并且极端的气候事件,例如干旱、洪水以及森林大火变得更加频繁。由于海平面上升,人口稠密的沿海地区及岛屿国家的无数的人们将失去他们的家园。在非洲、亚洲以及别的地区,贫穷的人们面临农作物歉收、降低的农业生产率以及日益增长的饥饿、营养不良和疾病等可能性。气候变化是我们这个年轻的世纪所面临的最复杂的挑战之一。此外这种变化需要我们现在就要行动起来并且一起行动起来。我们必须现在开始行动,因为我们今天所做的事情既决定未来的气候又决定塑造人类未来的选择。没有各国之间全球规模的合作,气候变化不可能得到解决。我们必须一起行动,因为气候变化是一场共同的危机。我们需要保护人类生命和生态资源。

我认为更多的事情需要人们去做。我们需要关于气候问题的行动,否则就来不及了。如果我们现在行动并且一起行动,真的有机会去为一个安全和可持续的全球化去塑造我们的气候未来。到2020年,中国将减少GDP每个单位二氧化碳排放量的40%~45%,以2005年为基线。我们无需等待一个低碳的未来。现在就开始吧。

重点写作词语点睛

sweat	v. 出汗	shape	v. 塑造
due to	由于	crisis	n. 危机
as	conj. 因为;随着	scale	n. 规模
shift	v. 变化	ecological	a. 生态的
prospect	n. 未来,前景	issue	n. 问题
malnutrition	n. 营养不良	globalization	n. 全球化
determine	v. 决定	low-carbon	低碳的

考研英语短文写作备考试题 第8篇

写作题目与要求

Study the following pie charts carefully and write an essay in which you should

1) describe the pie charts briefly,

2) explain their intended meaning, and then

3）give your comments.

You should write about 160~200 words neatly on ANSWER SHEET 2. （20 points）

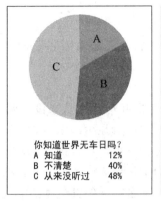 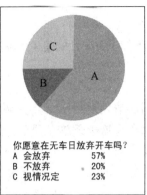

你知道世界无车日吗？
A 知道　　　　12%
B 不清楚　　　40%
C 从来没听过　48%

你愿意在无车日放弃开车吗？
A 会放弃　　　57%
B 不放弃　　　20%
C 视情况定　　23%

具体写作思路

1. 第一段的描述要反映两幅图中最重要的两个数字。
2. 第二段就人们缺乏国际环保知识和人们追求健康生活这两点分别进行阐述。
3. 第三段围绕普及环保知识和公众参与环保这两个方面陈述自己的看法。

参考范文

As is apparently revealed in the pie charts above, forty-eight percent of people surveyed have never heard of the International No Motor Vehicle Day while fifty-seven percent are willing to give up driving on such a day. What is betrayed in the pie charts is most thought-provoking.

The implied meaning of the pie charts is both disappointing and exciting. On the one hand, much necessary work still needs to be done with respect to environmental protection. The public ignorance of relevant environmental protection results from inadequate and limited popularity of environmental protection knowledge. Since environmental protection is an international issue, we must constantly introduce the advanced and practical practice in other countries to our general public. Only in this way can we promote environmental protection in China. On the other hand, the enhancement of the public awareness of environmental protection is a welcome development. Over the past years, as people's living standard improved, people attached more importance to the quality of their life. They have a better understanding of the relationship between environment and their daily life. As a result, they are more interested in following positive international models. In sum, we have got a mixed feeling toward the very fact revealed in the pie charts.

In my view, necessary measures should be immediately taken to ensure a nice environment. First of all, government departments at all levels must play a more active role in popularizing international experience and practice of environmental protection. What's more, the general public should be encouraged to _participate_ more actively in environmental protection. Only in these ways can we live in a healthy and harmonious environment. (271 words)

一句话点评

本文第二段针对环保知识重要性的阐述逻辑清晰，这一点恰恰是高分短文写作的基本要求。

全文翻译

如同上面的圆饼图所清楚地展示，接受调查的 48% 的人从来没有听说过国际无车日；同时，57% 的人愿意在无车日这一天放弃开车。圆饼图所显示的内容非常发人深省。

圆饼图的含义既令人失望又令人兴奋。一方面，就环境保护而言，必要的工作仍然需要去做。公众对于相关环境保护的无知是由于不充分的以及有限的环境知识的普及所造成的。因为环境保护是一个国际问题，所以我们应该不断地向公众介绍其他国家的先进和实用的方法，只有以这种方式，我们才能促进中国的环境保护。另外一方面，公众环保意识的加强是一种可喜的进步。近年来，由于人们生活水平的改善，人们更加重视生活的质量。他们更加理解环境和日常生活之间的关系。其结果是，他们对遵循积极的国际模式更加感兴趣。总之，对圆饼图中所展示的事实，我们有一种复杂的感觉。

我认为应该立即采取必要的措施以确保一个良好的环境。首先，各级政府部门应该在普及国际环保经验和办法方面起更加积极的作用。此外公众应该被鼓励更加积极地参与环境保护。只有以这两种方式，我们才能生活在一个健康和谐的环境中。

重点写作词语点睛

vehicle	_n._ 车辆	enhancement	_n._ 加强，提高
betray	_v._ 显示	awareness	_n._ 意识
with respect to	就…而言	welcome	_a._ 受欢迎的
ignorance	_n._ 无知	attach more importance to	更加重视
inadequate	_a._ 不充分的	follow	_v._ 遵循
constantly	_ad._ 不断地	ensure	_v._ 确保
practice	_n._ 惯例	popularize	_v._ 普及
promote	_v._ 促进，提高	participate	_v._ 参与

考研英语短文写作备考试题 第 9 篇

写作题目与要求

Study the following drawing carefully and write an essay in which you should

1) describe the drawing briefly,

2) explain the intended purpose of the painter, and then

3) give your comments.

You should write about 160 ~ 200 words neatly on ANSWER SHEET 2. （20 points）

——AH1N1

摘自《中国日报》

具体写作思路

1. 第一段的描述要反映人们积极主动地应对甲型 H1N1。
2. 第二段从科学性、法律以及中国国情的角度阐述积极应对甲型 H1N1 的正确性。
3. 第三段从政府和个人两方面应该采取的措施发表个人的观点。

参考范文

As is vividly displayed in the drawing above, a medical worker is fighting against A （H1N1） flu with the help of injection of vaccination. And the A （H1N1） flu is escaping from the resistance of our medical staff. What is conveyed in the drawing is worth discussing.

The aim of the painter can be interpreted as follows. Ever since the A （H1N1） flu began spreading across the world, the Chinese government has adopted timely and strict preventive measures. These measures are more than reasonable and necessary in the current situation. From the scientific viewpoint, there is still great uncertainty over the pathology and severity of the epidemic. Thus we are being cautious as "prevention is better than cure". From the legal viewpoint, China's actions are beyond reproach. According to China's Epidemic Prevention Law, suspected cases should be put under medical observation until confirmed. Faced with a spreading epidemic, China's measures are in conformity with the law and should be fully upheld. Moreover, the special conditions in China demand that strict control be exercised to prevent the outbreak of any epidemic disease. The density of population raises the risk more than in developed countries. Here, a couple of potential cases can impact a lot.

In my view, the government should use the 2003 SARS outbreak as an example to prepare for an eventuality. It should stop people from spreading rumors and causing unnecessary panic among the public. On an individual level, we should wash our hands often, avoid crowded places and cover our mouth and nose while sneezing. Above all, people should be told that A flu can be prevented and treated.

（275 words）

一句话点评

本文第二段从三个层面进行的相关分析和阐述条理十分清晰，这是高分短文写作所需要的重要能力之一。

全文翻译

如上面图画所生动地展示，一位医疗工作者正在借助于疫苗注射的方式与甲型 H1N1 流感作斗争。甲型 H1N1 流感正在从医疗人员的抵抗中逃跑。图画所传递的内容值得讨论。

图画作者的目的可以解释如下。自从甲型 H1N1 流感在全世界开始传播以来，中国政府已经采取了及时和严格的措施。这些措施在目前的情况下非常合理和必要。从科学的角度而言，这种流行病的病理和严重性有着很大的不确定性。因此我们是谨慎的，因为"预防胜于治疗"。从法律的角度而言，中国的行动无可指责。根据中国传染病防治法，疑似病例应该处于医学观察之下，直到被确定。面对传播的传染病，中国的措施符合法律并且应该充分得到支持。此外，中国特殊的情况需要实行严格的控制以避免任何流行疾病的爆发。与发达国家相比，人口的密度也提升了更大的危险性。在中国，若干可能的病例就能够影响许多人。

我认为政府应该利用 2003 年 SARS 的爆发作为例子，以便为不测事件做好准备。政府应该制止人们传播谣言以及在公众中造成不必要的惊恐。就个人而言，我们应该常洗手、避免去人多的场合、打喷嚏时要捂住嘴和鼻子。总之，应该告诉人们甲型 H1N1 流感是可防可治的。

重点写作词语点睛

injection	*n.* 注射	suspected	*a.* 疑似的
vaccination	*n.* 疫苗	observation	*n.* 观察
resistance	*n.* 抵抗	confirm	*v.* 确认
spread	*v.* 传播	in conformity with	与…一致
adopt	*v.* 采纳	uphold	*v.* 坚持
preventive	*a.* 预防性的	exercise	*v.* 施行
viewpoint	*n.* 观点	outbreak	*n.* 爆发
severity	*n.* 严重	density	*n.* 密度
epidemic	*n.* 传染病	rumor	*n.* 谣言
cautious	*a.* 谨慎的	panic	*n.* 惊恐
reproach	*n.* 指责	sneeze	*v.* 打喷嚏

考研英语短文写作备考试题　　第 10 篇

写作题目与要求

Study the following drawing carefully and write an essay in which you should

1) describe the drawing briefly,

2) explain its intended meaning, and then

3) give your comments.

You should write about 160~200 words neatly on ANSWER SHEET 2. (20 points)

——剽窃

摘自《中国日报》

具体写作思路

1. 第一段的描述要抓住剽窃这一现象。

2. 第二段从学术界的一贯风气和目前的状况展开论述和分析。

3. 第三段结合剽窃等行为所产生的不良影响发表个人的看法和观点。

参考范文

As is realistically depicted in the drawing above, an intellectual is quilting up his thesis by means of plagiarizing from books by other people. What is exposed in the drawing is not uncommon at present and should arouse the concern of our society.

The implication of the drawing can be interpreted as follows. For several thousands of years, academia has been considered as an ivory tower. Such fine qualities as spirit of dedication, hard work and perseverance have always been associated with intellectuals involved in academic study. A renowned ancient scholar tied his hair to the house beam to keep himself awake in order to learn more. Another one pricked his thigh with an awl every time he started dozing off. Such stories have inspired generations of scholars to devote themselves to higher learning. However, a national survey in the field of science and technology recently came up with a shocking result: almost half of the scholars polled claimed that plagiarism and fabrication are prevalent. Despite public anger over academic corruption, the cases of plagiarism exposed so far are only the tip of the iceberg. Writing dissertations is a way of training students on logical thinking and establishing their own creative argument. Imagine a world where degrees, diplomas, appraisals and professional titles could be obtained by means of cheating. What would it matter who you are?

In my view, cheating is dishonorable. Obviously, cheats have no respect for rules and for principles of fair play and justice. Can students who cheat be trusted not to cheat again, and again, in their lives? What of the damaging effect it has on the career and psyche of honest and diligent students? Those unscrupulous people are destructive to the future of this country. Therefore, something must be done to stop cheating. Now.   (297 words)

一句话点评

本文第二段对学术界一贯作风的描述使人心情久久不能平静，这种对比性的分析和表述方法是高分短文写作的有效手段之一。

全文翻译

如同上面图画所真实地描述，一位知识分子正在通过剽窃他人著作的办法来拼凑他的论文。本幅图画所揭露的内容在目前是常见的并且应该引起社会的关注。

本幅图画的含义可以解释如下。几千年以来，学术一直被人们认为是一座象牙塔。诸如献身、勤奋工作以及坚持不懈之类的优秀品质，一直与从事学术研究的知识分子联系在一起。为了学习更多的知识，一位古代著名的学者头悬梁使自己学习时保持清醒的状态。另外一位学者当自己打盹时就锥刺骨。这样的事例激励了一代又一代的学者投身于更高的学术研究。然而，最近一项全国范围的调查却提出了一项惊人的调查结果：近一半接受调查的学者宣称剽窃和造假是普遍的。尽管公众对学术腐败感到气愤，到目前为止所揭露的剽窃案件也仅仅是冰山一角。写论文原本是培养学者逻辑思维和建立自己创造性论点的一种方式。请大家想象一个这样的世界：通过作弊的手段人们可以得到学位、文凭、评价以及专业职称。如果这样，你是谁还重要吗？

我认为作弊是不诚实的。很明显，作弊者不尊重公平竞争和公正的原则。人们能够相信那些作弊的学者不在以后的人生中一次又一次地作弊吗？作弊对诚实和勤奋学者的事业和心理会产生什么样的破坏性影响？那些无耻的人对国家的未来是破坏性的。因此，我们一定要行动起来制止作弊。从现在开始吧。

重点写作词语点睛

intellectual *n.* 知识分子	academia *n.* 学术界
quilt up 拼凑	ivory tower 象牙塔
plagiarize *v.* 剽窃	quality *n.* 品质

dedication　*n.* 献身	argument　*n.* 论点
perseverance　*n.* 坚持不懈	degree　*n.* 学位
associate　*v.* 联系	diploma　*n.* 文凭
prick　*v.* 刺	appraisal　*n.* 评价
thigh　*n.* 大腿	matter　*v.* 有关系；要紧
doze off　打盹	dishonorable　*a.* 不诚实的
inspire　*v.* 激励	fair play　公平竞争
prevalent　*a.* 流行的，普遍的	justice　*n.* 公正
corruption　*n.* 腐败	psyche　*n.* 心灵
the tip of the iceberg　冰山一角	diligent　*a.* 勤奋的，用功的
dissertation　*n.* 论文	unscrupulous　*a.* 不讲道德的，无耻的

考研英语短文写作备考试题　　第 11 篇

写作题目与要求

Study the following drawing carefully and write an essay in which you should

1）describe the drawing,

2）analyze the aim of the painter of the drawing, and

3）give your example.

You should write about 160 ~ 200 words neatly on ANSWER SHEET 2.（20 points）

具体写作思路

1. 第一段对于图画的描述应该紧扣人与自然的关系。

2. 第二段的论述应该从保护自然资源和保护环境等方面展开。

3. 第三段的例子最好是最近发生的环保实例。

参考范文

As is <u>humorously</u> demonstrated in the drawing above, a man is shouldering a huge axe and intends to cut down the last tree of our <u>planet</u>. The tree can no longer <u>tolerate</u> the man's action and get ready to take its <u>revenge</u> on him. What is conveyed in the drawing reflects a reality and is most thought-provoking.

The main purpose of the painter can be interpreted in terms of <u>conserving</u> natural <u>resources</u> and protecting our environment. To begin with, natural resources should be conserved in order to keep <u>sustainable</u> development. It is well known that natural resources are limited. And some of them are not <u>renewable</u>. Thus, it is a must to make wise use of natural resources. In addition, excessive <u>exploitation</u> of natural resources must be prohibited so as to protect our environment. At present, it is a pervasive phenomenon that human beings are excessively exploiting natural resources including forest, oil, coal and gas. As a result, natural disasters such as flood and drought occur more frequently. And the <u>green-house</u> effect is becoming more serious. If we do not stop our irrational action, we will surely lose our only habitat and suffer severe <u>punishment</u> from the nature. In short, sustainable development calls for human efforts to conserve natural resources and protect our environment.

Take the gradual rise of sea level for example. It is a fact that the sea level is rising every year because of destruction of forest and <u>ozone layer</u>. If human beings do not reflect on the irrational action, tomorrow is surely the doomsday of mankind. To save ourselves, let's first protect our environment and conserve natural resources.

(273 words)

一句话点评

本文第一段对图画的描述准确且简练。

全文翻译

如图画幽默地显示，一个男人扛着一个巨大的斧子，并且想要砍伐我们星球上的最后一棵树。最后一棵树再也无法忍受这个男人的行为并且准备报复这个男人。图画所传达的信息反映了一种现实并且十分发人深省。

图画作者的目的可以从保护自然资源和保护我们的环境等方面加以解释。首先，应该保护自然资源以便保持可持续发展。众所周知，自然资源是有限的。并且其中一些资源是不能再生的。因此，合理利用自然资源是必需的。此外，一定要抑制过度开发和利用自然资源以便保护我们的环境。目前，普遍的现象是：人类过度开发和利用自然资源，包括森林、石油、煤和天然气。其结果，自然灾害，例如洪水和干旱，更频繁地发生。温室效应正在变得更加严重。如果我们不停止不理性的行为，我们将注定失去我们唯一的栖息地，并且承受大自然的惩罚。总之，可持续发展需要人类的努力来保护自然资源并且保护环境。

举海平面上升为例。人所共知：海平面每年都因为森林和臭氧层的破坏而上升。如果人类不反省其不理性的行为，明天就是人类的末日。为了拯救我们自己，让我们首先保护环境并且保护自然资源。

重点写作词语点睛

humorously *ad.* 幽默地	sustainable *a.* 可持续的
planet *n.* 星球	renewable *a.* 可再生的
tolerate *v.* 忍受	exploitation *n.* 开发，利用
revenge *n.* 报复	green-house *n.* 温室
conserve *v.* 保护；节约	punishment *n.* 惩罚
resource *n.* 资源	ozone layer 臭氧层

考研英语短文写作备考试题　第 12 篇

写作题目与要求

Study the following bar chart carefully and write an essay in which you should

1）describe the bar chart,

2）state the meaning, and

3）put forward your position.

You should write about 160~200 words neatly on ANSWER SHEET 2.（20 points）

大学生心中理想职业标准

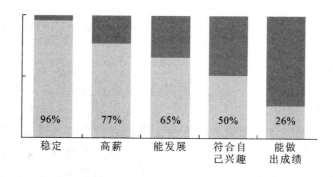

稳定	高薪	能发展	符合自己兴趣	能做出成绩
96%	77%	65%	50%	26%

具体写作思路

1. 对图表中的重要信息进行描述。

2. 从以下两个方面论述本图的含义：96% 的大学生追求"稳定"这一现象所暗示的含义；77% 和 65% 的大学生追求"高薪"和"能发展"这一现象所暗示的含义。

3. 从加强教育和创造健康环境提出自己的观点。

参考范文

As is apparently revealed in the bar chart above, steadiness, high salary and self-development are viewed as the ideal career standards by most university students. What is reflected in the chart is most thought-provoking and worth discussing among the general public for the time being.

The implied meaning which is conveyed in the bar chart can be briefly stated in the following two aspects. To begin with, the spirit of challenge is missing among most university students. As is indicated in the chart above, the majority of students regard steadiness as their top ideal career standard. The very fact shows that now most university students lack the confidence and courage to face hardships and difficulties in terms of work. What's more, most students are money-oriented and self-centered. As is indicated in the chart, high income and self-development are viewed as the most important factors in terms of their ideal career standards. The fact indicates that most people lack the spirit of serving the people and rewarding the society. In short, the employment ideal of university students needs to be adjusted.

In my view, some necessary measures should be taken to establish new ideal career standards among university students. On the one hand, a widespread education campaign must be launched to popularize correct employment concepts. On the other hand, a healthy social environment should be created so as to guide the development of students' mind. Only in these ways can university students find their ideal jobs in our harmonious society. (255 words)

一句话点评

本文根据图中所列出的实际数字进行阐述，对数字背后的含义理解深刻并且表达清晰。

全文翻译

如同上面的柱状图明确地显示，稳定、高薪和自我发展被看做是大多数大学生心中理想的职业标准。图中所反映的情况非常发人深省并且值得在公众中开展讨论。

上面图中所传递的深层含义可以从以下两个方面进行分析。第一，挑战的精神在大多数大学生中正在丧失。如同图中所示，大多数学生把稳定看做他们第一理想职业标准。这个事实显示现在大多数大学生缺乏面对工作中艰难困苦的自信和勇气。第二，大多数大学生向钱看并且以自我为中心。如图所示，高薪和自我发展被看做是他们理想职业目标的最重要因素。这个事实暗示大多数大学生缺乏服务人民回报社会的精神。总之，大学生的就业理想需要进行调整。

根据我的观点，应该采取一些必要的措施来确立新的理想职业标准。一方面，应该开展广泛的教育运动来普及正确的就业观念。另一方面，应该创造一个健康的社会环境以便引导学生的思想发展。只有以这些方法大学生才能够在我们的和谐社会中找到他们理想的工作。

重点写作词语点睛

be viewed as　被认为	reward　*v.* 回报
for the time being　目前	adjust　*v.* 调整
convey　*v.* 传递	popularize　*v.* 普及
hardship　*n.* 困苦	guide　*v.* 诱导
money-oriented　*a.* 向钱看的	harmonious　*a.* 和谐的

考研英语短文写作备考试题　　第 13 篇

写作题目与要求

Study the following drawings carefully and write an essay in which you should

1）describe the drawings briefly,

2）explain their intended meaning, and then

3）give your comments.

You should write about 160～200 words neatly on ANSWER SHEET 2. （20 points）

由"查找"到"搜索"——不仅仅是词汇上的变化

赵雪峰/绘画

具体写作思路

1. 第一段重点描写两幅图画中的鲜明变化与不同。

2. 第二段从改革开放和科学技术的巨变（含网络技术）等方面进行解释。

3. 第三段从教育和生活方面的变化进行拓展论述。

参考范文

It is well-known that one cannot put back the clock. As is realistically demonstrated in the drawings above, great changes have taken place with the passage of time. In the year of 2008, a young man was effortlessly searching online while in 1978 a scholar was working hard to hunt for materials among piles of books. What is conveyed in the drawings is both realistic and most meaningful.

The implied meaning of the drawings above can be interpreted in terms of the great changes and Reform and Opening-up. To begin with, great changes over the past 30 years should be attributed to the Reform and Opening-up since 1978. In 1978 China launched the Reform and Opening-up, which has greatly promoted the rapid growth of our national economy. The enhancement of our economy has brought about the robust development of science and technology including electronics. What's more, the development of science and technology has changed our way of study and work. Modern science and technology have brought us the most efficient means of work and study. More materials are available and much information can be obtained instantly and immediately by means of Internet and other hi-tech devices. The world is getting smaller and people are closer. In sum, thanks to the Reform and Opening-up, great changes have taken place over the past 30 years.

In fact, great changes have taken place in various aspects of our life besides science and technology. Over the past 30 years, education has had a great stride. College education is no longer a dream for the majority of young people. Our living standards have been greatly improved. We've got enough food and our clothes are more colorful. On the whole, great changes derive from the great policy and our constant efforts.　　　　　　　　　　(296 words)

一句话点评

本文第二段针对改革开放与科技发展（包括互联网）的论述条理分明且选词准确。

全文翻译

众所周知："时间不能倒流。"如上图真实所示，随着时间的推移，巨变已经发生。在 2008 年，一位年轻男子毫不费力地在网上搜索信息；而在 1978 年，一位学者正在费力地从书海中寻找资料。本图所传达的信息既真实又非常意味深远。

上面图画的深刻含义可以从改革开放和巨变等方面加以解释。首先，近 30 年来的巨变应该归因于自从 1978 年以来的改革开放。在 1978 年，中国开始了改革开放，这大大地推动了我们国家经济的快速发展。经济的加强带来了包括电子学在内的科技大发展。此外，科技发展改变了我们的工作和学习方式。现代科学技术给我们带来了最有效的工作和学习手段。通过互联网和其他高科技手段，我们可以迅速地获得更多的资料和大量的信息。世界变小了，人们的距离拉近了。总之，多亏了改革开放，近 30 年发生了巨大的变化。

实际上，除了科技，在我们生活的各个方面均发生了巨变。近 30 年以来，教育有了大发展。对于大多数年轻人来说，大学教育不再是一个梦想。我们的生活水平也大大地得到了改善。我们有足够的食物，我们的衣服也更加多姿多彩。总之，巨变来自于伟大的政策和不断的努力。

take place　发生	efficient　*a.* 有效的
effortlessly　*ad.* 毫不费力地	means　*n.* 手段
scholar　*n.* 学者	device　*n.* 装置
be attributed to...　被归因于…	thanks to...　多亏了…
bring about　产生	stride　*n.* 大步
robust　*a.* 强壮的	majority　*n.* 大多数

考研英语短文写作备考试题　　第 14 篇

写作题目与要求

Study the following drawing carefully and write an essay in which you should

1）describe the drawing,

2）analyze the aim of the painter of the drawing, and

3）state your view.

You should write about 160～200 words neatly on ANSWER SHEET 2. （20 points）

具体写作思路

1. 着重以"成功必经之路"为中心对图画进行描述。

2. 从以下两方面论述本图作者的主要目的：没有付出就没有收获；人们应该保持良好的心态。

3. 就开展广泛教育运动以及制定具体措施来发表自己的观点。

参考范文

As is vividly revealed in the drawing above, a man is asking himself which way to take.

The unavoidable way to success is teeming with cacti which represent hardship and challenge. What is conveyed in the drawing is most thought-provoking and worth discussing among the general public, especially young people.

The main purpose of the painter of the drawing can be briefly analyzed in the following two aspects. To begin with, "No pains, no gains" should always be our motto in our life and work. All of us are eager to be successful in whatever we do. However, some people are not industrious and try to find a short-cut to success. In fact, only those who are hard-working and brave enough to encounter difficulties of all sorts are most likely to reach the summit of success. What's more, an objective attitude should be maintained. In terms of our life, work and study, we will meet lots of trials. We must always face reality and have a second thought before we make our final decision. Success is also a process and needs to be realized step by step. As a proverb goes "Rome was not built in a day". In short, hard-working spirit and a realistic attitude lead to success.

In my view, some necessary measures should be taken so as for us to have a good understanding of success. On the one hand, a national education campaign should be launched to make people bravely face the reality. On the other hand, concrete plans should be made to help people realize importance of hard-working spirit. Only in these ways can we live in a harmonious and healthy society.

(277 words)

一句话点评

本文从辛勤劳动以及保持客观心态的角度出发进行论述是十分有说服力的。

全文翻译

如同上面的图画所逼真地显示，一个男人正在问自己选择走哪一条路。走向成功的必经之路充满荆棘，这些荆棘代表着成功到来之前的艰难困苦。图中所传递的信息非常发人深省并且值得我们在公众中，尤其是年轻人中展开讨论。

本幅图画作者的主要目的可以从以下两个方面进行简要分析。第一，"没有付出就没有收获"应该永远成为我们生活和工作中的座右铭。无论我们做什么，我们大家都渴望成功。然而，一些人并不勤奋，他们试图寻找一条走向成功的捷径。实际上，只有那些努力工作并且勇敢面对各种困难的人才有可能达到成功的顶点。第二，必须保持一个客观的心态。就工作、生活、学习而言，我们将遇到许多考验。我们一定要面对现实并且在我们做出最后决定之前要认真思考。成功也是一个过程并且需要一步一步地去实现。正如成语所说，"罗马非一日建成"。总之，努力工作的精神和现实主义的态度引领我们走向成功。

根据我的观点，应该采取一些必要的措施以便让我们对成功有充分的理解。一方面，应该开展全国性的教育运动使人们勇敢地面对现实。另一方面，应该制定具体的计划来帮助人们认识努力工作精神的重要性。只有以这些方式我们才能生活在一个和谐和健康的社会里。

teem with　充满

cactus　*n.* 仙人掌（*pl*）cacti

motto　*n.* 座右铭

industrious　*a.* 勤奋的

short-cut　*n.* 捷径

summit　*n.* 顶峰

trial　*n.* 考验

have a second thought　仔细想

process　*n.* 过程

concrete　*a.* 具体的

考研英语短文写作备考试题　　第 15 篇

写作题目与要求

Write an essay of 160 ~ 200 words based on the following drawing. In your essay, you should first describe the drawing, then interpret its meaning, and give your comment on it.

You should write neatly on ANSWER SHEET 2. （20 points）

座位

具体写作思路

1. 对图画里男女青年的占座行为进行描述，并引发主题讨论。

2. 从以下两方面论述该图画的含义：公共场合人们的行为举止有待提高；传统道德价值观有待加强。

3. 从加强教育和普及八荣八耻来提出自己的观点。

参考范文

As is vividly betrayed in the drawing above, a gentleman and a lady are sitting calmly on the <u>reserved</u> seats for babies and their mothers <u>while</u> a mother holding a baby in her arm is standing beside the seats. The drawing exposes a common social phenomenon and is most thought-provoking.

The implied meaning of the drawing is worth discussing. To begin with, manners should be improved in public places. Some people lack the necessary public awareness so that they pay no attention to the rules and regulations designed for public places. As a result, they disturb the normal order of public places. What's more, the traditional moral values should be enhanced. It is well known that to respect the elderly and take care of the young is one of our traditional virtues in our country. At present, some people are so selfish that they even neglect our traditional virtues in public places, which does no good to the healthy development of our society. In one word, we should make a deep reflection on our own deeds.

In my view, necessary measures should be immediately taken so as to create an ideal living environment. On the one hand, an education campaign should be launched to inform people of the acceptable and civilized manners in public places. On the other hand, "eight honors and eight disgraces" advanced by Hu Jintao should be publicized so as to enhance our sense of traditional virtues. Only in this way can we live in a harmonious society.　　(251 words)

一句话点评

该篇文章能将生活中的占座现象上升为八荣八耻的高度说明本文的作者有较高的思想觉悟。

全文翻译

如同上面图画所逼真地显示，一位男士和女士正平静地坐在为母婴所预留的座位上，而一位怀抱婴儿的母亲却站在座位的旁边。这幅图画揭示了一种常见的社会现象并且非常发人深省。

本幅图画的深层意义值得讨论。第一，应该改善公共场合的行为。一些人缺乏必要的公共意识以至于他们对为公共场合所制定的条规毫不在意。结果是，他们扰乱了公共场所的正常秩序。第二，应该加强传统的道德价值观。众所周知尊老爱幼是我们国家的传统美德。目前一些人十分自私以至于他们甚至在公共场所不顾传统美德，这对社会的健康发展没有好处。总之，我们应该对自己的行为进行深刻的反省。

根据我的观点，应该采取一些必要的措施以便营造一个良好的生活环境。一方面，应该开展教育运动以便告诉人们在公共场所可以接受的文明行为。另一方面，应该普及胡锦涛主席所提出的"八荣八耻"以便加强传统美德的观念。只有以这种方式我们才能生活在一个和谐的社会中。

重点写作词语点睛

reserved　*a.* 预留的	order　*n.* 秩序
while　*conj.* 而	virtue　*n.* 美德
awareness　*n.* 意识	reflection　*n.* 反省

56

design	*v.* 计划	deed	*n.* 行为
disturb	*v.* 打扰	eight honors and eight disgraces	八荣八耻

考研英语短文写作备考试题　　第 16 篇

写作题目与要求

Study the following drawing carefully and write an essay in which you should

1）describe the drawing briefly，

2）explain its intended meaning，and then

3）give your comments.

You should write about 160~200 words neatly on ANSWER SHEET 2.（20 points）

——30 年文化之变

赵斌/绘画

具体写作思路

1. 第一段重点描写图中孔子正在宣讲中国传统文化这一场面。

2. 第二段从改革开放和文化变迁等方面进行分析。

3. 第三段针对近 30 年的文化变迁所产生的益处发表自己的看法。

What a humorous and thought-provoking scene it is! As is vividly depicted in the drawing above, Confucius is standing on the platform, lecturing on Chinese traditional culture via the modern medium TV. What is conveyed in the drawing is both inspiring and meaningful.

The implied meaning of the drawing can be analyzed with respect to cultural changes and Reform and Opening-up. To begin with, the current cultural changes should be attributed to the Reform and Opening-up over the past 30 years. China launched Reform and Opening-up in 1978, which has promoted the rapid growth of national economy. The development of economy has brought about the great changes of culture, especially the traditional culture. What's more, the cultural changes are closely related to our pursuit of spiritual civilization. Over the past 30 years, much emphasis has been placed on the cultivation of spiritual civilization. The traditional cultural values are returning to our daily work, study and life. People become aware of the importance of such cultural virtues as responsibility, credibility and morality. Our minds are being enriched and guided by Chinese cultural values. In sum, great cultural changes have taken place in every aspect of our life.

In my view, great cultural changes over the past 30 years will benefit all Chinese. First of all, the cultural changes are conducive to the building-up a harmonious society. In addition, the international image can be elevated by the enhancement of our traditional culture.

(240 words)

一句话点评

本文第二段的相关论述紧扣"精神文明"这一论点，使本文主题十分鲜明。

全文翻译

这是多么幽默和发人深省的一幅场景啊！如上图生动所示，孔子站在讲台上，通过现代媒体电视宣讲中国传统文化。本图所传达的信息既激励人又意味深远。

本图的深刻含义可以从改革开放和文化变化等方面加以分析。首先，当前的文化变化应该归因于近30年以来的改革开放。1978年中国开始了改革开放，这推动了国民经济的迅速发展。经济的发展带来了文化巨变，尤其是传统文化。此外，文化变化与我们对精神文明的追求密切相关。在过去的30年里，我们十分重视精神文明建设。传统文化价值观回归于我们日常的工作、学习和生活。人们认识到责任、诚信和道德等文化美德的重要性。中国的文化价值观丰富并引导着我们的思想。总之，巨大的文化变化在我们生活的每个方面都已经发生了。

我认为近30年的文化巨变将有益于所有的中国人。首先，文化变化有益于构建和谐社会。此外，加强我们的传统文化能够提高我们的国际形象。

重点写作词语点睛

depict v. 描写

Confucius 孔子

via	*prep.* 通过	pursuit	*n.* 追求
medium	*n.* 媒体	spiritual civilization	精神文明
current	*a.* 目前的	virtue	*n.* 美德
be attributed to...	被归因于…	morality	*n.* 道德
bring about	带来，产生	conducive	*a.* 有益于
be closely related to...	与…关系密切	elevate	*v.* 提高

考研英语短文写作备考试题　　第 17 篇

写作题目与要求

Study the following pie chart carefully and write an essay in which you should

1）describe the pie chart,

2）analyze the purpose of the painter and

3）state your position.

You should write about 160 ~ 200 words neatly on ANSWER SHEET 2．（20 points）

哪种不文明行为最难接受？

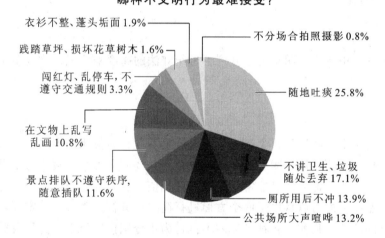

衣衫不整、蓬头垢面 1.9%

不分场合拍照摄影 0.8%

践踏草坪、损坏花草树木 1.6%

闯红灯、乱停车，不遵守交通规则 3.3%

随地吐痰 25.8%

在文物上乱写乱画 10.8%

不讲卫生、垃圾随处丢弃 17.1%

景点排队不遵守秩序，随意插队 11.6%

厕所用后不冲 13.9%

公共场所大声喧哗 13.2%

具体写作思路

1．对图中随地吐痰等重点不文明行为进行归纳和描述并且引出主题讨论。

2．从以下两方面对图画作者的目的进行讨论：应该对公共场所的不文明行为给予应有的注意；应该充分认识到不文明行为所产生的消极后果。

3．从加强全民教育运动和制定法规两个方面提出自己的观点和认识。

参考范文

Bad manners of various kinds in our daily life are apparently revealed in the pie chart above, among which spitting, littering, no flushing, and speaking loudly in public places are considered to be the most unacceptable of <u>uncivilized</u> manners. What is conveyed in the pie chart is most thought-provoking and worth discussing among the general public for the time being.

The main purpose of the painter of the pie chart can be briefly stated in the following two aspects. To begin with, bad manners in public places must be paid <u>due</u> attention. At present, bad manners of different sorts are so <u>rampant</u> in our daily life that the <u>order</u> of normal life is disturbed. If we neglect the very fact, the building of our harmonious society will be an empty talk. What's more, we should have a full understanding of the <u>negative</u> consequences of bad manners. It is reported that the bad manners of some Chinese tourists have already left a bad impression abroad. With the Beijing 2008 Olympic Games drawing near, each citizen of responsibility must make efforts to remove the bad manners. Otherwise, the international <u>image</u> of China would be severely <u>spoiled</u>. In short, joint efforts must be made to <u>get rid of</u> the <u>tumor</u> of bad manners.

In my view, some necessary measures must be made to <u>remove</u> the uncivilized manners. On the one hand, a national education campaign must be launched to inform people of the side-effects of bad manners. On the other hand, laws and regulations must be set up to punish those who perform bad manners. Only in these ways can we create a <u>disciplined</u> and harmonious society.

(274 words)

一句话点评

本文能够在写作中将不文明行为上升到不遵纪守法的高度来认识，这说明了文章作者的思想高度。

全文翻译

在上面的圆饼图中，我们日常生活中各种各样的不良行为被明确地揭示出来，在这些不良行为中，随地吐痰、乱丢垃圾、厕所用后不冲以及公共场所大声喧哗被认为是最不文明、最难以接受的行为。图中所传递的信息非常发人深省并且值得我们在公众中展开讨论。

图画作者的主要目的可以从以下两个方面进行简要的分析。第一，一定要对公共场所的不良行为给予应有的注意。目前，各种各样的不良行为十分猖獗以至于扰乱了我们的正常生活秩序。如果我们忽略这个事实，建立和谐社会将是一句空话。第二，我们应该充分认识不良行为的消极后果。据报道一些中国游客的不良行为已经在国外留下了不良的印象。随着北京2008年奥运会的到来，每一个有责任心的公民应该努力消除不良行为。否则，中国的国际形象将严重受损。总之，人们一定要共同努力来消除不良行为的毒瘤。

根据我的观点，一定要采取一些必要的措施以便消除不文明的行为。一方面，一定要开展全国性的教育运动来告诉人们不良行为的副作用。另一方面，一定要建立法规来惩罚那些从事不良行为的人。只有以这些方法我们才能营造一个有纪律的、和谐的社会。

重点写作词语点睛

manner *n*. 行为   uncivilized *a*. 不文明的

due	*a.* 应有的	get rid of	消除
rampant	*a.* 猖獗	tumor	*n.* 毒瘤
order	*n.* 秩序	remove	*v.* 消除
negative	*a.* 消极的	perform	*v.* 从事，做
image	*n.* 形象	disciplined	*a.* 有纪律的
spoil	*v.* 破坏		

考研英语短文写作备考试题　　第 18 篇

写作题目与要求

Study the following drawing carefully and write an essay in which you should

1）describe the drawing.

2）analyze the aim of the painter of the drawing, and

3）suggest counter-measures.

You should write about 160~200 words neatly on ANSWER SHEET 2.（20 points）

具体写作思路

1. 对图中两名大学生在食堂的浪费现象进行描述，再引发主题讨论。

2. 从以下两个方面对图画作者的目的进行论述：在校园里要培养学生勤俭节约的意识；要给予校园浪费应有的注意。

3. 从开展广泛的教育运动和建立法规两个方面提出自己的观点。

参考范文

As is vividly revealed in the drawing above, two students are dumping lots of their left-overs into big buckets in a university canteen. The phenomenon of wasting food on campus conveyed in the drawing is widespread and should arouse the concern of our society.

The main purpose of the painter of the drawing can be briefly analyzed in the following two aspects. To begin with, the sense of frugality needs to be cultivated on campus. Some students never think before they do and never care what they do. Though they are still not economically independent, they often spend spree. The wasting of food is just one of their wasting actions. As a result, the traditional virtue of frugality is being lost. What's more, due attention should be paid to the campus waste. Since some students fail to realize the importance of living a simple life, they unconsciously cause a great deal of waste in almost very detail of their actions. Campus wasting of food, water and power is alarming. Since our country is still a developing nation, such wasting poses a threat to the sustainable development of China. In short, the honor of frugality and simple life must be enhanced.

In my view, some necessary measures must be taken so as to reverse the grim campus situation. On the one hand, a wide spread education campaign should be launched to popularize the virtue of frugality. On the other hand, laws and regulations should be set up to punish those who waste. Only in these ways can we build up a harmonious and powerful China.

(264 words)

一句话点评

本文的写作紧紧围绕以艰苦奋斗为荣这一主题，这正是本文成功的关键所在。

全文翻译

如同上面图画所逼真地显示，两名学生正在把大量的剩余饭菜倒入大学食堂的大桶里。图画中所传达的这种大学校园浪费食物的现象是普遍的并且应该引起我们社会的关注。

本幅图画作者的主要目的可以从以下两个方面进行简要的分析。第一，节俭的意识应该在校园得到培养。一些学生在做事之前从不思考，对他们所做的事情也从不介意。虽然他们在经济上还没有独立，他们通常乱花钱。浪费食物只是他们浪费行为当中的一种，其结果是丧失了节俭的传统美德。第二，应该对校园浪费给予应有的注意。因为一些大学生没有认识到过俭朴生活的重要性，他们无意识地在他们行为中的每一个细节里造成了大量的浪费。校园中粮食、水和电的浪费是惊人的。由于我们国家仍然是一个发展中国家，这样的浪费对中国的可持续发展构成威胁。总之，节俭和俭朴生活的光荣观念应该得到加强。

根据我的观点，应该采取一些必要的措施以便扭转目前严峻的校园浪费形势。一方面，应该开展广泛的教育运动来普及节俭的美德。另一方面，应该建立法规来惩罚那些浪费的人。只有以这些方式我们才能建立一个和谐和强大的中国。

dump *v.* 倾倒	alarming *a.* 惊人的
left-overs *n.* 剩饭菜	pose *v.* 构成
frugality *n.* 节俭	sustainable *a.* 可持续的
spend spree 乱花钱	honor *n.* 光荣
unconsciously *ad.* 无意识地	reverse *v.* 扭转

考研英语短文写作备考试题　　第 19 篇

写作题目与要求

Study the following photo carefully and then write an essay of 160 ~ 200 words. In your essay, you should first describe the photo, then interpret its intended meaning, and give your example.

You should write neatly on ANSWER SHEET 2. (20 points)

具体写作思路

1. 第一段对图片的描述应该围绕大家积极参与志愿者的热情。
2. 第二段的解释和论述应该围绕奉献精神和社会工作等方面。
3. 第三段的实例最好是一个大家熟知的志愿者。

参考范文

　　As is vividly demonstrated in the photo above, several people are making their handprints on a <u>banner</u> of volunteers. Many people have already left their handprints or signed their names on the banner. What is conveyed in the photo is most meaningful and thought-provoking.

The implied meaning of the photo can be interpreted in terms of contribution and social work. In the first place, the contribution spirit of volunteers is needed to build up a harmonious society. As a social being, each of us get help from other people every day. In return, we should cultivate a sense of selflessness. In our daily life, we should try our best to contribute our love and care to our society. What's more, our social work can not be separated from volunteers' participation. China, as a developing country, still has much to be done. The students in the poverty-stricken area need volunteers. The senior citizens and AIDS patients need volunteers. Our environmental protection needs volunteers. At present, the 2008 Olympic Games also needs volunteers. In short, each of us should possess the noble spirit of volunteers and our society needs selfless volunteers.

Take Pu Cunxin for example. Pu is a famous actor in China. Unlike other stars, he gives up many money-making opportunities. In his spare time, he actively takes part in volunteer work. In particular, he often sends his care and love to AIDS patients. He sets us a shining example. We should learn from him and become volunteers so as to build up a harmonious society and live in world of care and love.

(264 words)

一句话点评

本文第三段所列举的实例十分贴近生活。

全文翻译

　　图片生动地描绘了这样的情景：一些人正在一面志愿者的旗帜上按下自己的手印。许多人已经在旗帜上留下了他们的手印或签署了自己的名字。图片所传达的信息耐人寻味并且发人深省。

　　图片的含义可以从奉献和社会工作等方面加以解释。首先，建立和谐社会需要奉献精神。作为社会中的人，我们每个人每天都从其他人那里得到帮助。我们应该确立无私的观念。在日常生活中，我们应该尽力向社会奉献关爱。此外，我们的社会工作需要志愿者的参与。作为一个发展中国家，中国仍然有许多事情要做。贫困地区的学生需要志愿者。老年人和艾滋病患者需要志愿者。我们的环境保护需要志愿者。目前，2008年的奥运会也需要志愿者。总之，我们每个人都应该具备志愿者的高尚精神，并且我们的社会需要无私的志愿者。

　　拿濮存昕为例。濮是一名著名的演员。与其他明星不同，他放弃了许多挣钱的机会。在业余时间，他积极参与志愿者工作。特别值得一提的是：他通常把关爱送给艾滋病人。他为我们树立了光辉的榜样。我们应该向他学习，成为志愿者以便建设和谐社会并且生活在关爱的世界里。

重点写作词语点睛

banner　n. 旗帜；横幅	participation　n. 参与
contribution　n. 奉献	poverty-stricken　a. 贫困的
harmonious　a. 和谐的	example　n. 榜样

写作题目与要求

Study the following drawing carefully and write an essay in which you should

1）describe the drawing briefly,

2）explain its intended meaning, and then

3）give your comments.

You should write about 160 ~ 200 words neatly on ANSWER SHEET 2. （20 points）

——爱如潮水

朱森林/绘画

具体写作思路

1. 第一段重点描写图中所反映的爱的暖流。

2. 第二段从大爱、团结和勇气等方面进行解释说明。

3. 第三段从汶川的未来这方面发表自己的看法。

参考范文

What a moving scene it is! As is vividly revealed in the drawing above, all Chinese people are actively making their share of donation for the victims in Sichuan earthquake to show their care, which forms a flood of great love. What is conveyed in the drawing is both inspiring and most meaningful.

The implied meaning of the drawing can be interpreted in terms of great love, unity and courage. First of all, blood is thicker than water. Great love is one of the essential virtues of our nation. Historically, whenever people in one region are hit by natural disasters, people living in other regions would lend their hands to dedicate their love and care, which is the core and nature of Chinese civilization. What's more, in unity there is strength. Unity is another essential and traditional virtue of our nation. Whenever we encounter hardships, Chinese of 56 nationalities would show more unity to face and overcome difficulties hand in hand and arm in arm. To Chinese, there is nothing to fear but fear itself. In sum, great love, unity and courage are the cornerstone of our national soul.

In my view, the future of Sichuan will be more promising. First of all, governments at different levels put much stress on the rehabilitation of earthquake-stricken areas. Besides, more love and care will constantly flow to Sichuan from people in different parts of our motherland. Most importantly, Sichuan people have a long history of wisdom, industriousness and bravery. Sichuan's tomorrow must be more attractive. (253 words)

一句话点评

本文第二段针对大爱与中华文明的论述贴近主题且十分感人。

全文翻译

这是多么感人的一幅图画啊！如上图生动所示，所有的中国人正在积极地为四川地震中的受难者做出自己的一份捐献来表达他们的关切之心，这形成了一股大爱之心的洪流。本图所传达的内涵既鼓舞人心又意义深远。

本图的深刻含义可以从大爱、团结和勇气等方面来诠释。首先，血浓于水。大爱是我们民族的重要美德之一。在历史上，每当一个地区的人们遭受自然灾害侵袭的时候，住在其他地区的人们总是会伸出他们的双手去奉献他们的爱和关心。这是中华文明的核心和本质。此外，团结就是力量。团结也是我们民族的一种重要的传统美德。每当遭遇艰难困苦，中国 56 个民族的同胞总是表现出更大的团结，手牵手、肩并肩去面对和克服困难。对中国人来说，除了惧怕本身，没有什么可惧怕的。总之，大爱、团结和勇气是我们民族灵魂的基石。

在我看来，四川的未来将更加充满希望。首先，各级政府部门更加重视地震灾区的重建。此外，更多的爱和关怀将源源不断地从祖国各地涌入四川。最重要的是四川人民有着悠久的历史，他们智慧、勤劳和勇敢。四川的明天一定会更加令人神往。

重点写作词语点睛

donation *n.* 捐款
care *n.* 关爱
inspiring *a.* 激励人的
unity *n.* 团结
virtue *n.* 美德
dedicate *v.* 奉献

core *n.* 核心
civilization *n.* 文明
nationality *n.* 民族
overcome *v.* 克服
cornerstone *n.* 基石
rehabilitation *n.* 恢复，重建

写作题目与要求

Study the following drawing carefully and write an essay in which you should

1）describe the drawing,

2）interpret the reason(s) for the case,

3）suggest counter-measures.

You should write about 160～200 words neatly on ANSWER SHEET 2.（20 points）

具体写作思路

1. 围绕 2048 年餐桌上就不会有鱼了对图画进行描述。

2. 从以下两个方面对图中现象进行解释：一直以来对鱼的过度捕捞；越来越严重的污染。

3. 从加强教育和建立法规两个方面提出自己的观点和看法。

参考范文

As is vividly revealed in the drawing above, a man is imagining what a fish looks like. The announcement in the drawing reads "There will not be fish on our table in the year 2048". What is conveyed in the drawing is most thought-provoking and sounds an alarm for every citizen on the earth.

The main reasons for the extinction of fish can be analyzed in the following two aspects. First of all, over-fishing is the No. 1 killer. Traditionally, people lack a scientific understanding of ocean and fish species. In order to obtain huge profits, over-fishing has become a common phenomenon. As a result, the ecological system of the ocean and sea has been severely ruined. What's more, pollution is increasingly damaging habitats of various fish species. As the global industry and economy develop rapidly, pollution is getting more serious than ever before. Much waste and poisonous water are discharged into the oceans and seas, which destroys the habitats of fish. As a consequence many ocean creatures die off. In short, over-fishing and pollution result in the extinction of many fish species.

In my view, some necessary measures should be immediately taken to avoid the prediction in the drawing. On the one hand, an international education campaign must be launched to make people know the importance of protecting fish resources. On the other hand, relevant laws and regulations should be established to reverse the grim situation and protect ocean creatures. Only in these ways can we live in a harmonious environment and enjoy delicious fish for good. (256 words)

一句话点评

本文第二段所指出的过度捕捞和污染这两个原因真实而具体，使本文充实并且具有说服力。

全文翻译

如同上面图画所逼真地显示，一个男子正在想象鱼是什么样子。图中的公告中提示"2048 年餐桌上就不会有鱼了"。图中所传递的内容非常发人深省，并且为地球上的每一位公民敲响了警钟。

鱼类灭绝的主要原因可以从以下两个方面进行分析。第一，过度捕捞是头号杀手。一直以来，人们缺乏对海洋和鱼类的科学理解。为了获得巨大利润，过度捕捞已经成为一种常见的现象。其结果，海洋的生态系统被严重破坏。第二，污染越来越严重地破坏各种鱼类的栖息地。随着全球工业和经济的迅速发展，污染比以往任何时候都变得更加严重，许多废水和毒水被排入江河湖海，这破坏了鱼类的栖息地。其结果，许多海洋生物消亡了。总之，过度捕捞和污染导致了许多鱼类的灭亡。

根据我的观点，应该立即采取一些必需的措施以便避免图画中的预言。一方面，应该开展国际性的教育运动以便使人们了解保护鱼类资源的重要性。另一方面，应该制定相应的法规来扭转目前严峻的形式并且保护海洋生物。只有以这些方法我们才能生活在一个和谐的环境中并且永远享用到美味的鱼。

重点写作词语点睛

announcement   n. 通知，公告

sound an alarm   敲响警钟

extinction   n. 灭绝

over-fishing   （鱼类的）过度捕捞

ecological   a. 生态的

habitat   n. 栖息地

discharge   v. 排放

as a consequence   其结果

creature   n. 生物

die off   消亡

avoid　*v.* 避免　　　　　　　　　　delicious　*a.* 美味的

resource　*n.* 资源

考研英语短文写作备考试题　　第 22 篇

写作题目与要求

Study the following drawing carefully and write an essay in which you should

1) describe the drawing,

2) interpret the meaning of the drawing, and

3) state your suggestion.

You should write about 160 ~ 200 words neatly on ANSWER SHEET 2. (20 points)

极品月饼 绘画/黎青

具体写作思路

1. 第一段对于图画的描述应该紧扣有关月饼的事实。

2. 第二段的论述要从中国传统文化和商业利润等方面展开。

3. 第三段中的建议应该切实可行。

参考范文

As is vividly revealed in the drawing above, a man opens a box of <u>moon cake</u> and to his surprise, there are two big bottles of wine in it and the moon cakes are incredibly small. This is <u>ridiculous</u> but it reflects a social fact which is most thought-provoking.

The intended meaning of the drawing can be interpreted in terms of <u>commercial</u> profit and traditional Chinese culture. First of all, it seems that our market is flooded with <u>money-</u>

orientedness. Businessmen in every field try their best to make as much <u>profit</u> as possible without caring the social effect of their <u>conducts</u>. Making-money has become their top <u>priority</u>, which is <u>detrimental</u> to the business credibility. What's more, it appears that our traditional culture is disappearing. With the rapid development of our society, our traditional festivals should be rejuvenated with creative improvements. In general, the irrational desire of commercial profit should be <u>curbed</u> and our traditional festivals must be protected with modern wisdom.

In my view, <u>counter-measures</u> should be taken so as to reverse the current grim fact mentioned above. To begin with, laws and regulations should be established in order to <u>regulate</u> our business market. In addition, special efforts should be made by every responsible citizen of our society to make sure our traditional festivals develop and shine in our modern time. In sum, we should be aware that our traditional culture is being destroyed by money-orientedness and something must be done without <u>delay</u>. 　(242 words)

一句话点评

本文第二段的论述完整地表达了图画的深层含义。

全文翻译

如同图画所生动地提示，一个人打开一盒月饼。使他大吃一惊的是：里面有两大瓶酒，里面的月饼非常小。这种现象是荒谬的，但是却反映了一种普遍的社会现象，并且十分发人深省。

图画的含义可以从商业利润和中国传统文化两个方面加以解释。首先，我们的市场似乎都在向钱看。各个领域的商人尽其所能获取利润，而不介意其行为的社会影响。赚钱成为他们的头等大事，这种情况对商业诚信是有害的。此外，传统文化似乎正在消失。由于社会的迅速发展，应该用创造性的改进来振兴传统的节日。总之，商业利润的不合理欲望应该得到抑制，并且一定要用当代的智慧保护我们的传统节日。

根据我的观点，应该采取应对措施以便扭转目前严峻的现实。首先，应该立法来管理我们的商业市场。另外，我们社会每个负责任的公民应该做出特殊的努力以确保我们的传统节日在当代发扬光大。总之，我们应该认识到：我们的传统文化正遭到向钱看的损害，并且人们一定要刻不容缓地做一些事情。

重点写作词语点睛

moon cake 月饼	priority *n.* 优先考虑的事
ridiculous *a.* 荒谬的	detrimental *a.* 有害的
commercial *a.* 商业的	curb *v.* 抑制
money-orientedness 向钱看	counter-measure 应对措施
profit *n.* 利润	regulate *v.* 管理
conduct *n.* 行为	delay *n.* 延误

写作题目与要求

Study the following drawing carefully and write an essay in which you should

1）describe the drawing briefly,

2）explain its intended meaning, and then

3）give your example（s）.

You should write about 160 ~ 200 words neatly on ANSWER SHEET 2.（20 points）

——目标

摘自《解放军报》

具体写作思路

1. 第一段重点描写图中军人的大目标和小目标

2. 第二段主要从人生目标、耐心和坚持等方面进行解释。

3. 第三段以邓亚萍为例说明。

参考范文

　　It is well-known that "Great oaks from little acorns grow". As is vividly demonstrated in the drawing above, a PLA soldier has set himself a goal and then divided the goal into small but concrete targets so as to carry out his plan step by step. What is conveyed in the drawing is most instructive and thought-provoking.

　　The implied meaning of the drawing can be interpreted with respect to the goal of life, patience and persistence. To begin with, it should be realized that nothing seek, nothing find. As a social being, self-development is of importance. A definite goal, which is based on personal interests and abilities, must be set up so as to make our ideal come true. What's more, we should bear the proverbs in mind that "Rome was not built in a day" and "Every little makes". Nothing could be achieved overnight. And to achieve one's goal is no exception. It needs a process and <u>constant</u> efforts. In sum, drops of water outwear the stone.

Take Deng Yaping for example. Deng is a super table-tennis player and has <u>snatched</u> numerous gold medals in international events. However, it is hardly known that Deng began her training when she was four years old. It is Deng's sweat, tears, patience and persistence that have helped her <u>achieve</u> her goal. As a saying goes: "Slow but steady win the race".

(229 words)

一句话点评

本文第二段所使用的多处谚语是本文的闪光点和得分点。

全文翻译

众所周知："合抱之木始于毫末"。正如上图生动所示，一名解放军战士为自己确定了一个目标，然后又把这个目标划分为小的，但却是具体的目标，以便一步一步地实现自己的计划。本图所传达的信息非常富有教育意义并且发人深省。

本图的深刻含义可以从人生目标、耐心和坚持等方面加以解释。首先，我们应该认识到：没有追求就没有成就。作为社会中的一个人，自我发展是重要的。基于个人兴趣和能力的明确目标一定要确立起来，以便使我们的理想实现。此外，我们应该牢记这两个谚语："罗马非一日建成"和"积少成多"。任何事情不可能一蹴而就。达到我们的目标也不例外。这需要一个过程和不断地努力。总之，滴水穿石。

以邓亚萍为例。邓亚萍是一位超级乒乓球运动员，并且摘得无数国际比赛的金牌。但是，鲜为人知的是：邓亚萍四岁时就开始训练了。恰恰是邓亚萍的汗水、泪水和坚持帮助她达到其目标。常言道："稳扎稳打，无往不胜。"

重点写作词语点睛

PLA soldier	解放军战士	ideal n.	理想
goal n.	目标	exception n.	例外
concrete a.	具体的	constant a.	不断的
persistence n.	坚持	snatch v.	摘得
definite a.	明确的	achieve v.	达到

考研英语短文写作备考试题　第24篇

写作题目与要求

Study the following drawing carefully and write an essay in which you should

1) describe the drawing briefly,

2) explain the intended aim of the painter, and then

3）give your choice.

You should write about 160~200 words neatly on ANSWER SHEET 2.（20 points）

——选择

郝廷鹏/绘画

具体写作思路

1．第一段重点描写图中金鱼都奔向大城市这一现象。

2．第二段从牺牲精神和明智的选择等方面进行解释。

3．第三段以去西部工作说明自己的个人选择。

参考范文

What a humorous and thought-provoking drawing it is! As is vividly revealed in the drawing, nearly all the goldfish jump into the big <u>tank</u> which is labeled with the word "<u>metropolis</u>" so that they face <u>fierce</u> competition and <u>cruel</u> survival condition. No fish is willing to stay in small towns and <u>countryside</u>. What is conveyed in the drawing is realistic and most meaningful.

The main purpose of the painter can be briefly interpreted in terms of <u>wise</u> choice and the spirit of <u>devotion</u>. To begin with, <u>discretion</u> is the better part of choice. It is no doubt that the metropolis is <u>intriguing</u> with respect to our career and self-development. However, when a metropolis is over-crowded with talents, we need to have a second thought in making a choice. We also need to be aware of the old sayings that "One man's meat is another man's <u>poison</u>" and "Every man has his price." Therefore the place that suits us should be the best and wise choice for us. What's more, the spirit of devotion should be <u>enhanced</u> among young <u>talents</u>. It must be recognized that self-development and our career can not be <u>separated</u> from the growth of our <u>motherland</u>. Without the growth of small towns and the vast rural areas, China can not develop. As a modern talent, we must combine our personal

73

pursuit with the development of our nation in making career choice. In sum, both wise choice and the spirit of devotion should be taken into account in choice-making.

As far as I am concerned, the West is my top choice. First of all, I was born and grew up there so that I intend to start my career in the West. Besides, as a student of agronomy, it is my duty to take roots in the rural area of the West.

(296 words)

一句话点评

本文第二段第二点针对奉献精神的论述反映了当代大学生的风采。

全文翻译

这是多么幽默且发人深省的一幅图画啊！如上图生动所示，几乎所有的金鱼都跳入大鱼缸。这个鱼缸上贴有一枚标签，上面写着"大城市"。这样一来，他们面临激烈的竞争和残酷的生存环境。没有鱼儿愿意呆在小城镇和农村。本图所传达的信息真实且非常耐人寻味。

本图作者的主要目的可以从明智的选择和奉献精神两个方面简要地加以解释。首先，慎重是选择的重要组成部分。毫无疑问，就我们的事业和个人发展而言，大城市是非常吸引人的。但是，当大城市人才人满为患时，我们在做出选择时需要三思。我们还需要认识到这两句古语："对甲有利的，未必对乙有利"和"人各有其价"。因此，适合于我们的地方应该是我们最佳、最明智的选择。此外，奉献精神应该在青年人才中得到加强。人们应该认识到：个人的发展以及我们的事业是无法与祖国的发展相分离的。没有小城镇和广大农村地区的发展，中国就无法发展。作为一名当代人才，在做出事业的选择时，我们一定要把个人的追求和国家的发展结合起来。总之，在做出抉择时，应该对明智选择和奉献精神这两点加以考虑。

就我而言，西部是我的首选。首先，我在那里出生并且长大，所以我想在西部开始我的事业。此外，作为一名主修农学的学生，在西部农村地区扎根是我的责任。

重点写作词语点睛

tank *n.* 鱼缸	poison *n.* 毒药
metropolis *n.* 大城市	enhance *v.* 加强
fierce *a.* 激烈的	talent *n.* 人才
cruel *a.* 残酷的	separate *v.* 分离
countryside *n.* 农村	motherland *n.* 祖国
wise *a.* 明智的	pursuit *n.* 追求
devotion *n.* 奉献	take... into account 考虑
discretion *n.* 慎重	the West 西部
intriguing *a.* 吸引人的	take roots 扎根

写作题目与要求

Study the following drawing carefully and write an essay in which you should

1）describe the drawing briefly,

2）explain the intended purpose of the painter, and then

3）give your comments.

You should write about 160～200 words neatly on ANSWER SHEET 2.（20 points）

——侵占

赵国品/绘画

具体写作思路

1. 第一段重点描述大量农田被侵占这一现实。
2. 第二段从城市发展和粮食供给等方面进行分析。
3. 第三段从保护农田和避免粮食危机等方面提出自己的看法。

参考范文

As you sow, so shall you reap. As is humorously revealed in the drawing above, a crane is being utilized to construct buildings. The buildings are invading more and more farming land which provides us with grain. Consequently our rice bowl will be spoiled and food crisis is inevitable. What is conveyed in the drawing is most meaningful and thought-provoking.

The aim of the painter can be analyzed in terms of urban development and food supply. First of all, a rational plan must be made with respect to urban development. With the increase of population, urban sprawling runs rampant and farming land is turned into residential areas. New buildings are erected by each passing day. Random invasion of farming land must be immediately stopped. What's more, the sense of farming land protection must be cultivated. We cannot survive without food. Food crisis can lead to many social problems. It can destroy social <u>stability</u> and even <u>ignite</u> war. In sum, random urban sprawling can no longer be neglected and the protection of farming land is a must.

In my view, urgent <u>measures</u> need to be made and taken so as to protect farming land and avoid food crisis. On one hand, a nation-wide education campaign should be launched to raise the public's <u>awareness</u> of protecting faming land. On the other hand, laws must be set up to punish those who destroy farming land. Only in these ways can we keep sustainable development.

(241 words)

一句话点评

本文第二段针对"侵占"这一主题的论述有理有据,说服力极强。

全文翻译

种瓜得瓜,种豆得豆。正如上图幽默所示,人们正在使用吊车建造楼房。楼房正在侵占越来越多的供给我们粮食的农田。其结果,我们的饭碗将遭到破坏,并且粮食危机不可避免。本图所传达的信息非常耐人寻味并且发人深省。

本图作者的目的可以从城市发展和粮食供给等方面加以分析。首先,就城市发展而言,人们一定要制定合理的计划。由于人口的增长,城市扩张失控了,农田变成了住宅区。每天人们都在建造新的楼房。人们一定要立即停止对农田的任意侵占。此外,保护农田的意识一定要得到培养。没有食物,我们无法生存。粮食危机能够导致许多社会问题。危机可以破坏社会稳定,甚至引发战争。总之,人们不能再忽略任意的城市扩张,农田保护是一定要做的事情。

我认为,我们需要制定并且采取迫切的措施以便保护农田并且避免粮食危机。首先,人们应该开展一场全国范围的教育运动以便提高公众保护农田的意识。另一方面,我们应该立法来惩罚那些破坏农田的人。只有以这些方法,我们才能保持可持续发展。

重点写作词语点睛

sow	v. 播种	residential	a. 居住的
reap	v. 收获	erect	v. 建造
crane	n. 吊车	random	a. 随意的
utilize	v. 使用	invasion	n. 侵入
bowl	n. 碗	cultivate	v. 培养
urban	a. 城市的	stability	n. 稳定
rational	a. 合理的	ignite	v. 点燃,引发
sprawling	n. 扩张	measure	n. 措施
rampant	a. 无节制的	awareness	n. 意识

写作题目与要求

Study the following drawing carefully and write an essay in which you should

1) describe the drawing,

2) interpret the meaning of the drawing, and

3) state your suggestion.

You should write about 160 ~ 200 words neatly on ANSWER SHEET 2. （20 points）

具体写作思路

1. 第一段对于图画的描述应该紧扣人们齐心协力的精神。

2. 第二段的论述要从合作、奉献和和谐社会等方面展开。

3. 第三段中的建议和措施应该具体并切实可行。

参考范文

As is vividly revealed in the drawing above, four people are making joint efforts to finish a beautiful painting, which shows that a family is living happily in the sun. What is indicated in the drawing above is most meaningful and thought-provoking.

The implied meaning of the drawing can be interpreted in terms of cooperation, contribution and harmonious society. On the one hand, cooperation and contribution are needed in our society. Every person should have a sense of responsibility to contribute to our society. Learning to cooperate and contribute is indispensable to all the people. On the other hand, harmonious society is built up by means of joint efforts of the general public. It should be generally <u>recognized</u> that the happiness of our own life depends largely on the cooperation and contribution made by other people. We can not live without care and love which are offered by people surrounding us. In one word, we need cooperation and contribution in pursuit of a harmonious society and life.

In my opinion, some necessary measures must be taken to <u>ensure</u> the establishment of a harmonious society. First of all, an education campaign should be launched so as to <u>guide</u> every citizen to <u>cultivate</u> a sense of contribution and cooperation. What's more, government departments at different levels must work hard to make people realize that an ideal living environment is created through joint efforts. Only in these ways can we live in a <u>harmonious</u> society.

（243 words）

一句话点评

本文第二段的论述层次分明、条理清楚且选词得当。

全文翻译

如同图画所生动地展示，四个人正在共同努力来完成一幅美丽的图画。图画显示一个家庭幸福地生活在阳光下。图画所暗示的信息意味深长并且十分发人深省。

图画的含义可以从合作、奉献以及和谐社会等方面来解释。一方面，我们社会需要合作和奉献。每个人都应该具有责任感以便为社会作出贡献。学会合作和奉献对于所有的人都是不可或缺的。另一方面，和谐社会是通过公众的共同努力构建起来的。人们应该广泛认识到：我们个人的幸福依赖于其他人所做出的合作和奉献。没有其他人所奉献的关爱，我们就无法生存。总之，我们在追求和谐社会和生活中需要合作和奉献。

根据我的观点，应该采取必要的措施以确保和谐社会的构建。首先，应该开展教育运动以便引导每个公民培养奉献和合作的意识。此外，各级政府部门一定要努力工作以便使我们认识到：理想的生活环境是通过共同努力创造的。只有以这些方式，我们才能生活在一个和谐的社会里。

重点写作词语点睛

in the sun	在阳光下	recognize	v. 认可
cooperation	n. 合作，配合	ensure	v. 确保
contribution	n. 奉献	guide	v. 引导
responsibility	n. 责任	cultivate	v. 培养
indispensable	a. 不可缺少的	harmonious	a. 和谐的
by means of	通过		

写作题目与要求

Study the following bar chart carefully and write an essay in which you should

1）describe the bar chart,

2）state the meaning, and

3）put forward your position.

You should write about 160 ~ 200 words neatly on ANSWER SHEET 2.（20 points）

自愿无偿献血

我国自愿无偿献血占采集临床用血比例

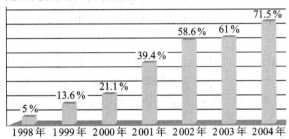

摘自《新京报》

具体写作思路

1. 对图表所传达的重要信息进行描述，尤其是有关 2004 年的数字。

2. 从以下两方面论述本图的含义：精神文明的进步；对健康知识的了解。

3. 从普及公众教育和立法两方面提出自己的观点。

参考范文

　　As is obviously revealed in the bar chart above, over the past seven years（1998—2004）, the proportion of free blood donation in clinical blood collection has been climbing and rocketed to over seventy percent in 2004, which is a welcome development to our whole society.

　　The implied meaning of the bar chart above can be illustrated as follows. To begin with, the increasing percentage indicates that great changes have taken place in terms of people's spiritual civilization. Most people want to make contribution to our society in one way or another while they are getting help from others. More and more people deem that to do a bit for others is a way to realize self-value. The spirit of selflessness is more pervasive than ever before. What's more, the statistics betray that modern people, especially the young, have a better understanding of medical knowledge. Most people have abandoned their old idea that blood donation is most harmful to human body. In one word, our spiritual progress and rich medical knowledge have resulted in such a positive result.

In my view, effective measures should be taken to encourage free blood donation. First of all, a nation-wide education campaign should be launched to spread the necessity and knowledge of free blood donation. Besides, laws should be set up to protect those who donate blood. Only in this way can we create a harmonious and healthy society. (234 words)

一句话点评

本文从精神文明方面入手进行深刻的论述，重点突出。

全文翻译

如同上面的柱状图所明确显示的一样，在过去的 7 年里（1998—2004），自愿无偿献血占采集临床用血的比例一直在增长，并且在 2004 年激增到 70% 以上。这对全社会而言是一个可喜的发展。

上面的柱状图所表达的含义可以阐述如下。首先，日益增长的比例表明了人们精神文明方面所发生的巨大变化。当大多数人得到别人帮助的同时，他们想要以一种方式或另一种方式为社会作贡献。越来越多的人认为：为别人做一点事情是实现自我价值的一种方式。无私的精神比以往任何时候都更加普遍。此外，统计数字表明，现代人，尤其是年轻人，对医学知识有了更深刻的理解。大多数人放弃了他们过时的观念——献血对身体是非常有害的。总之，我们的精神进步和丰富的医学知识产生了这种积极的结果。

根据我的观点，应该采取行之有效的措施以便鼓励自愿无偿献血。首先，应该开展一个全国性的教育运动以便传播无偿献血的必要性和知识。此外，应该确立相应的法律来保护那些献血的人。只有以这种方法我们才能创造一个和谐和健康的社会。

重点写作词语点睛

proportion	n. 比例	self-value	自我价值
free blood donation	无偿献血	selflessness	n. 无私
rocket	v. 激增	pervasive	a. 普遍的
civilization	n. 文明		

考研英语短文写作备考试题　　第28篇

写作题目与要求

Study the following drawing carefully and write an essay in which you should

1）describe the drawing briefly,

2）explain the intended purpose of the painter, and then

3）give your example（s）.

You should write about 160～200 words neatly on ANSWER SHEET 2.（20 points）

——短跑健将的双腿

金凤官/绘画

具体写作思路

1. 第一段重点描写图中残疾运动员奋力拼搏的动人场景。
2. 第二段从自信、勇敢和拼搏等方面进行解释。
3. 第三段以张海迪为例进行说明。

参考范文

It is well-known that "God helps those who help themselves". As is vividly revealed in the drawing above, a disabled athlete is running with all his efforts. Without legs, he is running with the spirit of struggling and courage. What is conveyed in the drawing above is both inspiring and instructive.

The main purpose of the painter above can be interpreted in terms of self-confidence, bravery and the spirit of struggling. To begin with, it should be recognized that "Nothing is impossible to a willing heart." In our daily life, work and study, we often encounter hardships and difficulties. And sometimes our task is really demanding. Only self-confidence can help us tide over difficulties. What's more, it should be realized that "Fortune favors the brave". In our routine life and work, we will meet with insurmountable difficulties. Occasionally we do feel helpless and fall in desperate situation. In this case, to be or not to be depends on whether we have enough courage to struggle. Only by the spirit of struggling can we have a silver lining. In sum, self-confidence, bravery and the spirit of struggling is the chord of life.

Take Zhang Haidi for example. Zhang was paralyzed with high fever when she was a little girl. However, she did not give up her life. She learned English from radio and later translated and published a novel entitled *Seaside Clinic*. Besides she has been active in the social work for the disabled and was elected president of the National <u>Association</u> of the Disabled of PRC. Zhang has set a good example for all of us. We should "Never say die".

(273 words)

一句话点评

本文第一段首句和第三段尾句所使用的谚语和名言是本文的点睛之笔。

全文翻译

众所周知："自助者天助。"正如上图生动所示，一名残疾运动员正在全力以赴向前奔跑。没有双腿，他正在用拼搏和勇气向前跑。本图所传达的信息既激励人又有教育意义。

本图作者的主要目的可以从自信、勇敢和拼搏精神等方面加以解释。首先，人们应该认识到："有志者事竟成。"在我们的日常生活、工作和学习中，我们经常遇到艰难困苦。有时，我们的任务十分艰巨。只有自信能够帮助我们克服困难。此外，人们应该认识到："勇者事成。"在日常生活和工作中，我们将遇到无法克服的困难。有时我们的确感到无助并且陷入绝望的境地。在这种情况下，何去何从取决于我们是否拥有足够的勇于拼搏的勇气。只有通过拼搏，我们才能拥有一线光明。总之，自信、勇敢和拼搏的精神是人生之弦。

以张海迪为例。她很小的时候因高烧而瘫痪。但是，她没有放弃生命。她从收音机里学习英文并且翻译出版了《海边诊所》这本小说。此外，他还一直积极参与残疾人的社会工作，并且被选为中国残疾人联合会的主席。张海迪为我们树立了好榜样。我们应该"永不言败"。

重点写作词语点睛

disabled	*a.* 残疾的	insurmountable	*a.* 无法克服的
struggle	*v.* 拼搏	desperate	*a.* 绝望的
demanding	*a.* 苛刻的	to be or not to be	是活着还是死去
tide over	度过	a silver lining	一线光明
fortune	*n.* 命运	paralyze	*v.* 使瘫痪
routine	*a.* 日常的	association	*n.* 联合会

考研英语短文写作备考试题　第 29 篇

写作题目与要求

Study the following pie charts carefully and write an essay in which you should

1) describe the pie charts, and

2) deduce the meaning of the pie charts above, and

3) make a comment.

You should write about 160 ~ 200 words neatly on ANSWER SHEET 2. (20 points)

具体写作思路

1. 对两幅图中的重要信息进行描述，尤其是有关诚信度和工作经验。

2. 从诚信度和工作经验两个方面阐述图表的含义。

3. 从"诚实为上策"和提前进行就业准备两个方面说明自己的观点。

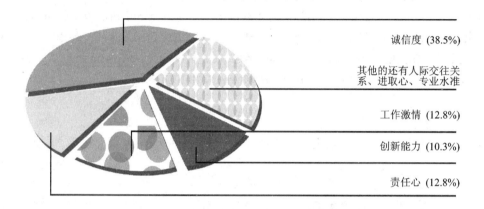

用人单位对应届毕业生的素质要求

诚信度 (38.5%)

其他的还有人际交往关系、进取心、专业水准

工作激情 (12.8%)

创新能力 (10.3%)

责任心 (12.8%)

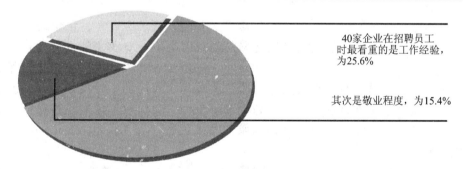

用人单位对普通员工的素质要求

40家企业在招聘员工时最看重的是工作经验，为25.6%

其次是敬业程度，为15.4%

摘自《法制晚报》

参考范文

As is apparently betrayed in the pie charts above, credibility and working experience are the twin leading quality requirements for college graduates and ordinary working staff by most working units. The very fact is most thought-provoking and worth discussing with the competition in labor market getting more fierce than ever before.

The implied meaning of the pie charts above can be briefly stated as follows. To begin with, it is necessary for job-hunters to realize the importance of credibility in terms of job-hunting. At present, most people simply concentrate all their attention on their professional training while neglecting the <u>shaping</u> of their credibility. In fact, it is well-known that credibility is the foundation of our work and life. What's more, it is high time that job-hunters <u>consciously</u> <u>accumulated</u> some working experience before they look for a job. Since working experience has become a deciding factor in job-hunting, job-hunters had better grasp any opportunity to enrich their relevant professional experience. For instance, university students may <u>take advantage of</u> their holidays and vacations to practice in relevant working units, which can enhance their <u>competitiveness</u> in job market. In sum, credibility and working experience should not be neglected by job-hunters.

In my view, some measures should be taken to strengthen our competitiveness in terms of job-hunting. On the one hand, we had better always bear in mind the <u>motto</u> "Honesty is the best policy". On the other hand, we should make necessary <u>adjustments</u> in the preparation for job-hunting. Only in these ways can we find a job that we want.　　(259 words)

一句话点评

本文围绕两幅图中的重要信息进行重点的剖析，层次鲜明，论述颇具说服力。

全文翻译

如同上面的圆饼图所明确揭示的一样，诚信和工作经验是大多数工作单位对大学毕业生和普通员工的两个主要素质要求。这个事实发人深省并且值得讨论，因为目前劳动市场的竞争比以往任何时候都更加激烈。

上面两幅圆饼图的深层含义可以被简述如下。首先，就求职而言，认识到诚信的重要性是非常必要的。目前，大多数人仅仅把他们的注意力集中在专业培训上而忽略了诚信的塑造。实际上，众所周知，诚信是我们工作和生活的基础。此外，求职者在找工作之前应该有意识地积累一些工作经验。因为工作经验已经成为求职时的一个决定因素，所以求职者最好抓住任何机会来丰富自己相关的专业经验。例如，大学生可以利用自己的节假日到相关工作单位去实践，这样能够增强他们在求职市场的竞争力。总之，诚信和工作经验不应该被求职者所忽略。

根据我的观点，人们应该采取一些措施来加强自己在求职方面的竞争力。一方面，我们最好一直牢记这个座右铭："诚实为上策"。另一方面，我们应该在求职准备方面做出必要的调整。只有以这样的方式我们才能找到一份我们想要做的工作。

重点写作词语点睛

betray	v. 显示	accumulate	v. 积累
credibility	n. 诚信	take advantage of	利用
quality	n. 素质	competitiveness	n. 竞争力
shape	v. 塑造	motto	n. 座右铭
consciously	ad. 有意识地	adjustment	n. 调整

写作题目与要求

Study the following pie chart carefully and write an essay in which you should

1）describe the pie chart,

2）analyze the reasons, and

3）state your plan.

You should write about 160~200 words neatly on ANSWER SHEET 2.（20 points）

具体写作思路

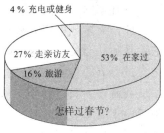

1. 对图中所提供的重要信息进行描述，尤其是大多数人过春节方式的信息。

2. 从以下两个方面谈论现象的原因：春节的传统概念；人们重视亲戚关系。

3. 根据个人情况具体阐述自己的计划。

（制图：耿争）

参考范文

As is obviously revealed in the pie chart above, Chinese people spend the Spring Festival in different ways. The majority of the people surveyed enjoy the holiday together with their family members at home, while twenty-seven percent of the people surveyed visit their relatives and friends to share the happiness of the Spring Festival. The popular ways to enjoy the holiday reflect our national culture and tradition.

The foremost reasons why most people choose to spend the holiday at home or to visit their relatives or friends can be illustrated as follows. To begin with, in China, the Spring Festival means the get-together of all the family members. No matter where one lives and works, he would try his best to go back home when the holiday is coming. Therefore, it is quite natural that most Chinese would like to enjoy the holiday together with their family members at home. What's more, Chinese have always treasured their kinship and social inter-relationship. That accounts for the choice of the twenty-seven percent of the people surveyed—to visit their relatives and friends. In one word, the important ways to spend the Spring Festival are permeated with our culture and tradition.

As far as I am concerned, I plan to spend the Spring Festival together with my family members this year. Owing to my financial status and study project, I spent the last two Spring Festivals at university. At that moment, I was quite homesick. As soon as my exam is over, I will start my journey to my home. As a proverb goes, "East or west, home is the best." (268 words)

一句话点评

本文用极其简洁的语言精确地论述了文化传统方面的重要性，写作思路清晰。

全文翻译

如同上面的饼状图所明确显示的一样，中国人过春节的方式各有不同。被调查的大多数人在家里和家人一起过春节，而另外接受调查的百分之二十七的人走亲访友过春节。过春节的大众方式反映了我们民族文化和传统。

大多数人在家里过春节或走亲访友过春节的主要原因可以阐述如下。首先，在中国，春节意味着所有家庭成员的团聚。无论人们生活或工作在什么地方，人们会争取在春节到来时回家。因此，大多数中国人喜欢在家里和家人一起过春节是很自然的事。其次，中国人一直珍视亲戚关系和社会关系。这就解释了接受调查的百分之二十七的人的选择——走亲访友过春节。总之，过春节的重要方式充满了我们的文化和传统。

就我而言，我计划今年和家人一起过春节。由于我的经济状况和学习计划，我在大学度过了最近两年的春节。此时，我很想家。考试一结束，我将踏上回家的旅程。俗话说："金窝银窝不如自己的草窝。"

重点写作词语点睛

the Spring Festival	春节	kinship	*n.* 亲戚关系
majority	*n.* 大多数	account for	解释
get-together	团聚	permeate	*v.* 充满
treasure	*v.* 珍视	homesick	*a.* 想家的

考研英语短文写作备考试题　　第 31 篇

写作题目与要求

Study the following bar chart carefully and write an essay in which you should

1）describe the bar chart briefly,

2）explain the main reason（s）, and then

3）give your comments.

You should write about 160~200 words neatly on ANSWER SHEET 2.（20 points）

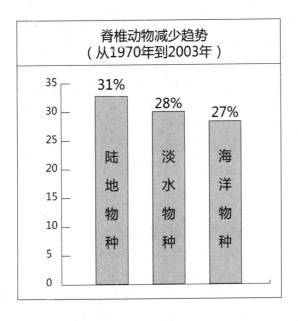

——脊椎动物减少趋势

具体写作思路

1. 第一段重点描写三种物种的具体减少趋势。
2. 第二段从过度捕猎、过度捕捞和污染等方面进行解释。
3. 第三段从教育和立法等方面提出自己的看法。

参考范文

What a shocking fact it is! As is accurately demonstrated in the bar chart above, vertebrate species decreased steeply from 1970 to 2003, with terrestrial species, fresh water species and marine species declining 31, 28 and 27 percent respectively. What is conveyed in the chart is alarming and thought-provoking.

The main causes for the sharp decrease can be interpreted in terms of over-hunting, over-fishing and pollution. To begin with, over-hunting and over-fishing have resulted in the decline of vertebrate species. As the global population is increasing, it poses a threat to vertebrate species. People view vertebrate species as the main source of meat. It is apparent that the number of vertebrate is bound to dive due to population explosion and the resulting over-hunting and over-fishing. What's more, pollution has also led to the drop of vertebrate species. With the rapid growth of economy, one factory after another is built all over the world. Consequently, many terrestrial species have lost their habitat. Modern industry also bring with it pollution. Factories discharge much waste water into river, lake, sea and ocean, thus contaminating the water on which freshwater and marine species depend. In sum, destructive activities of human being have led to the diving of vertebrate species.

In my view, necessary moves must be taken without any delay so as to protect vertebrate species. On one hand, a world-wide campaign should be launched to raise the public's awareness of protecting vertebrate species. On the other hand, laws and regulations must be set up to punish those who hurt vertebrate species. Only in these ways can we keep sustainable development.

(267 words)

一句话点评

本文第一段针对柱状图表的描述全面细致且十分准确。

全文翻译

这是多么令人震撼的一个事实啊！正如上图精确所示，从 1970 年到 2003 年，脊椎动物急速减少。陆地物种、淡水物种和海洋物种分别下降 31%、28% 和 27%。本图所传达的信息令人担心并且发人深省。

脊椎动物急剧减少的主要原因可以从过度捕猎、过度捕捞和污染等方面加以解释。首先，过度捕猎和过度捕捞造成脊椎动物的减少。由于全球人口的增长，人口对脊椎动物构成了威胁。人们把脊椎动物视为肉食的主要来源。显然，由于人口爆炸和随之而来的过度捕猎和过度捕捞，脊椎动物的数量注定急剧减少。此外，污染也导致了脊椎物种的减少。由于经济的迅速发展，人们在世界各地修建了一个又一个工厂。其结果，许多陆地物种失去了栖息地。现代工业也带来了污染。工厂将大量的废水排入河流、湖泊和海洋，因此污染了淡水和海洋物种赖以生存的水源。总之，人类破坏性的活动导致了脊椎动物的急剧减少。

我认为：我们应该立即采取必要的措施以便保护脊椎动物。一方面，我们应该开展世界范围的运动来提高公众保护脊椎动物的意识。另一方面，我们应该确立法律法规以便惩罚那些伤害脊椎动物的人。只有以这些方式，我们才能保持可持续发展。

重点写作词语点睛

accurately *ad.* 精确地	dive *v.* 急速下降
bar chart 柱状图	explosion *n.* 爆炸
decline *v.* 下降	discharge *v.* 排放
cause *n.* 原因	contaminate *v.* 污染
pose a threat to... 对…构成威胁	destructive *a.* 破坏的
view... as 把…看做	move *n.* 措施
source *n.* 来源	campaign *n.* 运动，战役
be bound to... 注定…	sustainable *a.* 可持续的

写作题目与要求

Study the following pie chart carefully and write an essay in which you should

1）describe the pie chart,

2）analyze the reasons for the leading advocacy, and

3）state your position.

You should write about 160 ~ 200 words neatly on ANSWER SHEET 2. （20 points）

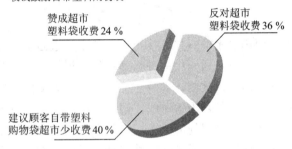

"自带塑料购物袋应少收钱"

近5 000人参与调查，四成受调查者建议以少
收钱鼓励自带塑料购物袋

赞成超市
塑料袋收费24 %

反对超市
塑料袋收费36 %

建议顾客自带塑料
购物袋超市少收费40 %

（制图：程强）

具体写作思路

1. 对图表中所提供的重要信息进行描述，尤其是大多数人所坚持的观点。

2. 从以下两方面讨论主流意见的原因：白色污染问题；节约自然资源。

3. 从普及教育和消费者付费两个方面提出自己的观点。

参考范文

As is obviously betrayed in the pie chart above, forty percent of the people surveyed advocate that customers should bring plastic bags with themselves when they do shopping in the super-market, which mirrors a strong consciousness of environmental protection among ordinary people in China.

The foremost reasons for the advocacy revealed in the pie chart above can be illustrated as follows. To begin with, our planet is worsening by each passing day due to the pollution caused by human beings. Wherever you go, especially the places along the railway, white pollution resulting from plastic bags is ubiquitous. We can no longer wait and see. What's more, to protect the natural resources is our duty. If we do not practice strict economy, what will be left to our offsprings? This is also a moral topic. The typical plastic bags are not disposable items. So we should make full use of them. On the whole, the environmental protection, the idea of economy, and our social obligation have contributed to the advocacy of self-brought plastic bags.

In my view, measures should be taken to promote the leading advocacy. In the first place, a nation-wide campaign should be launched to educate people, especially the young, how to understand the relationship between human beings and our environment. Besides, customers should pay for the plastic bags. In sum, to protect our environment, we should not neglect the white pollution.

(233 words)

一句话点评

本文把一个小小的题目推到一个环保和道德的高度，重点突出，用词准确。

全文翻译

如同上面的饼状图所明确显示的一样，接受调查的百分之四十的人提倡在超市购物时顾客应该自带塑料袋。这反映了中国普通人中一种强烈环保意识。

上面饼状图所倡导的原因可以被阐述如下。第一，由于人类所产生的污染，我们的星球每天都在恶化。无论走到哪里，尤其是沿铁路线，塑料袋所产生的白色污染随处可见。我们不能再观望了。第二，保护自然资源是我们的义务。如果我们不厉行节约，我们将留给后代什么？这还是一个道德话题。一般的塑料袋不是一次性物品。因此我们应该充分利用它们。总之，环境保护、节约观念和社会义务促成了提倡自带塑料袋的行为。

我认为，应该采取措施促进这一主流倡议。首先，一场全国性的运动应该被开展以便教育人们，尤其是年轻人，如何理解人类和自然的关系。此外，顾客应该为塑料袋付钱。总之，为了保护环境，我们不应该忽略白色污染。

重点写作词语点睛

advocate v. 提倡   ubiquitous a. 无处不在的
plastic bag 塑料袋   resource n. 资源
consciousness n. 意识   practice strict economy 厉行节约
white pollution 白色污染   disposable a. 一次性的

考研英语短文写作备考试题　第33篇

写作题目与要求

Study the following table carefully and write an essay in which you should

1) describe the table,

2）analyze the meaning, and

3）suggest counter-measures.

You should write about 160~200 words neatly on ANSWER SHEET 2. （20 points）

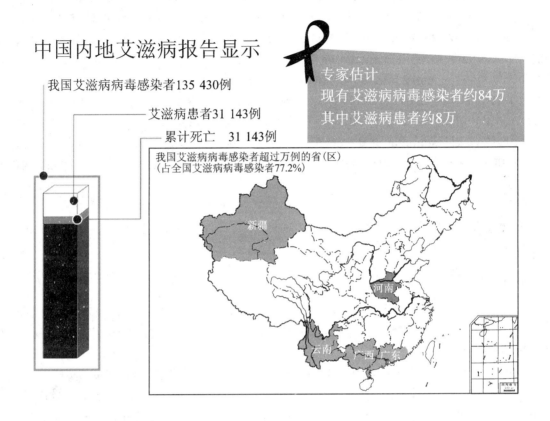

中国内地艾滋病报告显示

我国艾滋病病毒感染者135 430例

艾滋病患者31 143例

累计死亡 31 143例

专家估计
现有艾滋病病毒感染者约84万
其中艾滋病患者约8万

我国艾滋病病毒感染者超过万例的省(区)
(占全国艾滋病病毒感染者77.2%)

具体写作思路

1. 对图中所提供的重要信息进行描述，尤其是现有艾滋病病毒感染者人数以及我国艾滋病病毒感染者超过万例的省（区）。

2. 从以下两个方面讨论本图的含义：艾滋病的控制和预防。

3. 从法律和公共教育提出应对措施。

参考范文

As is accurately revealed in the drawing above, the number of HIV carriers in China is estimated at 840,000 and about 77 percent of HIV/AIDS cases are in Yunan, Henan, Xinjiang, Guangxi and Guangdong. The current grim situation is most thought-provoking and worth discussing for the time being.

The implied meaning of the drawing above can be briefly stated as follows. To begin with, it is high time that we realized the necessity of AIDS control, especially in some provinces. Over the past years, the number of AIDS cases and HIV carriers is on the rise. If no effective measures are taken immediately, the number of HIV carriers in our country could increase to 10 million in 2010. What's more, it is imperative that we should realize the importance of AIDS prevention. AIDS prevention is an issue related to the quality of the population, economic development, social stability and the rise or decline of our nation. In sum, AIDS control and prevention should be put on our agenda.

In my view, counter-measures should be taken to reverse the grim situation. On the one hand, relevant laws and regulations should be set up by government to control the spread of AIDS. On the other hand, a public education campaign should be launched to make people have a better understanding of the epidemic and the relevant knowledge of AIDS prevention. Only in these ways can we stop AIDS and live in a harmonious society. （242 words）

一句话点评

本文从图表的重要数字入手非常深刻地剖析了数字后面所暗示的内容，层次鲜明，用词十分准确。

全文翻译

如同上面的图表所准确地揭示的一样，我国 HIV 携带者的数量估计在 84 万人，并且 HIV 艾滋病例的 77% 集中在云南、河南、新疆和广东四个省（区）。目前的严峻现实发人深省并且值得展开讨论。

上面图表的深层含义可以被简述如下。首先，我们应该认识到遏制艾滋病的必要性，尤其是在一些省（区）。近年来，艾滋病病例和 HIV 携带者的数量呈上升趋势。如果不立即采取有效的措施，到 2010 年我国 HIV 携带者的数量可能增长到 1000 万人。此外，重要的是我们应该意识到预防艾滋病的重要性。预防艾滋病与人口的素质、经济的发展、社会稳定和民族的兴衰息息相关。总之，遏制和预防艾滋病应该放到我们的议事日程上来。

根据我的观点，我们应该采取应对措施来扭转目前严峻的现实。一方面，应该确立相应的法规以便遏制艾滋病的传播。另一方面，应该开展一场公众教育运动以便让人们更好的理解这种传染病以及相应的预防艾滋病的知识。只有以上述方式我们才能遏制艾滋病并生活在一个和谐的社会里。

重点写作词语点睛

carrier	*n.* 携带者	agenda	*n.* 议事日程
grim	*a.* 严峻的	counter-measure	*n.* 应对措施
thought-provoking	发人深省的	reverse	*v.* 扭转
necessity	*n.* 必要性	epidemic	*n.* 传染病
imperative	*a.* 迫切的	harmonious	*a.* 和谐的

写作题目与要求

Study the following bar chart carefully and write an essay in which you should

1）describe the bar chart briefly,

2）explain the major reason(s), and then

3）give your comments.

You should write about 160 ~ 200 words neatly on ANSWER SHEET 2. （20 points）

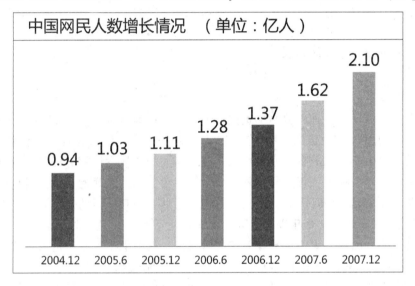

具体写作思路

1. 第一段重点描述图中我国网民增长的总体趋势。

2. 第二段从改革开放和科技发展等方面进行解释。

3. 第三段从政府重视和百姓意识等方面对未来趋势发表个人的看法。

参考范文

What an amazing trend it is! As is accurately revealed in the bar chart above, the number of Chinese netizens was climbing from 2004 to 2007, with the number reaching 210 million in 2007. What is demonstrated in the chart is both encouraging and most meaningful.

The main reasons for the apparent increase of Chinese netizens can be interpreted in terms of science and technology and the Reform and Opening-up. To begin with, science and technology have created a new world. Over the past years, great changes have taken place in the field of science and technology. Internet is the symbol of information era, which connects the world and considerably improves the efficiency of our life, work and study. What's more, Reform and Opening-up has broadened Chinese people's horizon. Since 1978, great progress has been made not only in the living standards but also in the liberation of our mind. More people have recognized the importance of information and efficiency. As a result, Internet has entered both our office and home. In sum, the growth of science and the improvement of our mind contribute to the increase of Chinese netizens.

In my view, the trend of netizen increase will continue in China. On one hand, our government places more stress on the integration with the world and the wide application of modern technology. On the other hand, Chinese are becoming more aware of the significance of information. The day when netizen means citizen is around the corner.　　（250 words）

一句话点评

本文第一段针对柱状图的描述突出了重点信息内容。

全文翻译

这是多么令人惊讶的一种趋势啊！正如以上柱形图精确所示，从 2004 年至 2007 年，中国网民的人数一直增加，2007 年的人数高达 2.1 亿。本图传达的信息既激励人又意味深长。

中国网民人数明显增加的主要原因可以从改革开放和科技发展等方面加以解释。首先，科技创造了一个新世界。在近些年，科技领域发生了巨大变化。互联网是信息时代的标志，互联网把全世界联结在一起，并且大大地提高了我们生活、工作和学习的效率。此外，改革开放拓宽了中国人的视野。自从 1978 年以来，人们不仅在生活水平而且在思想解放方面都取得了巨大的进步。更多的人已经认识到信息和效率的重要性。其结果，互联网进入了我们的办公室和家庭。总之，科学的发展和思想的进步促进了中国网民的增加。

我认为网民增加的趋势将在中国持续。一方面，我们的政府更加重视与世界的融合以及现代技术的广泛应用。另一方面，中国人民更加认识到信息的重要性。网民也就是公民的那一天就要到来了。

重点写作词语点睛

netizen　n. 网民　　　　　　　　　　horizon　n. 视野

climb　v. 上升　　　　　　　　　　liberation　n. 解放

in the field of...　在…领域　　　　contribute to...　促成…

Internet　n. 互联网　　　　　　　　trend　n. 趋势

symbol　n. 象征　　　　　　　　　place more stress on...　更加重视…

era　n. 时代　　　　　　　　　　　integration　n. 融合

considerably　ad. 大大地　　　　　application　n. 应用

efficiency　n. 效率　　　　　　　　be around the corner　即将到来

broaden　v. 开阔

94

写作题目与要求

Study the following drawing carefully and write an essay in which you should

1）describe the drawing,

2）analyze the aim of the painter of the drawing, and

3）suggest counter-measures.

You should write about 160~200 words neatly on ANSWER SHEET 2. （20 points）

发展与环境

具体写作思路

1. 对图中所提供的重要信息进行描述，尤其是 GDP 的增长和污染。

2. 从以下两方面讨论本图作者的目的：盲目追求 GDP 的增长对环境的破坏；GDP 的增长和生态环境之间的关系。

3. 从立法和公共教育两个方面提出应对措施。

参考范文

As is vividly betrayed in the drawing above, people are striving for the tremendous increase of GDP（gross domestic product）at the cost of our environment. The blue sky is being severely polluted and human life is being threatened, which is most thought-provoking and worth discussing among the general public for the time being.

The main purpose of the painter of the drawing above can be briefly stated as follows. To begin with, it is high time that we realized the fact that our living environment and some natural resources are being destroyed in the blind pursue of GDP increase. At present, the ecology of our planet can hardly support the continuous expansion of heavy-polluting, high-consuming and low-profit production pattern. What's more, it is quite necessary that we have an objective understanding of the relationship between GDP increase and the ecological environment. The GDP increase which is achieved at the cost of sacrificing human living environment and destroying our valuable natural resources (some of the resources are not renewable) is meaningless at all. In sum, the blind craze for GDP increase must be stopped.

In my view, counter-measures should be taken to reverse the grim situation. On the one hand, relevant laws and regulations must be set up by government to ensure a rational balance between GDP increase and our living environment. On the other hand, a public education campaign should be launched to make people have a good knowledge of green GDP. Only in these ways can we have a sustainable development and a harmonious society.

(257 words)

一句话点评

本文从盲目追求 GDP 的增长和重视生态环境两个方面层次鲜明地围绕主题进行剖析，用词贴切。

全文翻译

如同上面的图画所逼真地显示的一样，人们以牺牲环境为代价努力追求 GDP 的巨大增长。蓝色的天空被严重污染，人类的生命受到威胁，这一切发人深省并且值得现在在公众中展开讨论。

上面图画作者的主要目的可以被简述如下。首先，我们应该认识到这一事实：在盲目追求 GDP 增长的同时，我们的生存环境和一些自然资源被毁掉。目前我们地球的生态几乎不能支撑高污染、高消耗和低效益生产模式的持续扩张。此外，必要的是我们应该对 GDP 的增长和生态环境之间的关系有一个客观的理解。以牺牲人类生存环境并且破坏我们宝贵的自然资源（一些资源是不能再生的）为代价所取得的 GDP 增长是毫无意义的。总之，人们必须制止对 GDP 增长的盲目狂热。

根据我的观点，应该采取应对措施来扭转目前的严峻形势。一方面，应该确立相应的法规以确保 GDP 增长和生存环境之间的合理平衡。另一方面，应该开展一场公众的教育运动以便使人们更好的理解绿色 GDP。只有以上述方面我们才能拥有一个可持续发展的和谐社会。

重点写作词语点睛

betray	v. 显示	sacrifice	v. 牺牲
strive	v. 努力	craze	n. 狂热
threaten	v. 威胁	rational	a. 合理的
blind	a. 盲目的	sustainable	a. 可持续的
ecology	n. 生态	harmonious	a. 和谐的

写作题目与要求

Study the following drawing carefully and write an essay in which you should

1）interpret the drawing,

2）analyze the meaning of the drawing, and

3）state your view.

You should write about 160 ~ 200 words neatly on ANSWER SHEET 2.（20 points）

具体写作思路

1. 对图中所提供的重要信息进行描述，尤其是有关日常生活节水的信息。

2. 可从以下两个方面谈论本图的含义：树立节约的观念和公共参与节约行动。

3. 从全民公共教育和政府参与两个方面提出自己的观点。

参考范文

　　As is vividly revealed in the drawing above, water is being wisely <u>utilized</u> in the daily life of a family. The good <u>conduct</u> is indeed praiseworthy and should be <u>popularized</u> in our society.

　　The implied meaning of the drawing can be stated as follows. To begin with, to practise economy is closely related to our daily life. In terms of our clothing, food, sheltering, and transport, much work can be done to save valuable energy and natural resources such as power, water, coal, gas and so on. We, as university students, should take the wise use of paper and second-hand textbooks into consideration. What's more, the public <u>participation</u> is the foundation of a society in which to practise economy is advocated and treasured. Since social environment is <u>shaped</u> by the general public, the <u>cultivation</u> of <u>conservation-minded society</u> depends on the active <u>involvement</u> of every member of our society, be he old or young. In sum, our daily life should be <u>permeated</u> with the sense of practising economy and public participation should be encouraged.

In my view, necessary measures should be taken so as to practise economy. On the one hand, we should launch a public campaign to help people build up the sense of practicing economy in our <u>routine</u> life. On the other hand, education on how to practise economy must be promoted by relevant government departments and professionals at different levels. Only in this way can we create a real conservation-minded society.　　　　(243 words)

一句话点评

本文围绕本题的核心（日常节约）进行深刻的论述，用难易得当的语言阐述重要观点。

全文翻译

如同上面的图画所逼真地展现的一样，在一个家庭的日常生活中水被合理地利用。这种良好的行为的确值得表扬并且应该在我们社会中得到普及。

上面图画的深层含义可以被简述如下。首先，厉行节约与我们日常生活密切相关。就我们的衣食住行而言，可以做许多工作以便节约宝贵的能源和自然资源，例如：电、水、煤、气等等。作为大学生，我们应该考虑合理利用纸张和旧书。此外，公共参与是提倡厉行节约社会的基础。因为社会环境是由公众所塑造的，所以节约型社会的培养依赖于我们社会每个成员的积极参与，无论是年老的还是年轻的。总之，我们的日常生活应该充满厉行节约的意识，并且公共的参与应该得到鼓励。

根据我的观点，必要的措施应该采取以便厉行节约。一方面，我们应该开展一场公共运动以便帮助人们逐步树立日常生活中厉行节约的意识。另一方面，有关如何厉行节约的教育应该得到有关政府部门和各级专业人士的促进。只有以上述方式我们才能创造一个真正的节约型社会。

重点写作词语点睛

utilize　*v.* 利用	cultivation　*n.* 培养
conduct　*n.* 行为	conservation-minded society　节约型社会
popularize　*v.* 普及	involvement　*n.* 参与
participation　*n.* 参与	permeate　*v.* 充满
shape　*v.* 塑造	routine　*a.* 日常的

写作题目与要求

Study the following drawing carefully and write an essay in which you should

1）describe the drawing briefly，

2）explain its intended meaning，and then

3）give your comments.

You should write about 160~200 words neatly on ANSWER SHEET 2.（20 points）

——枯竭

摘自巴拿马《快报》

具体写作思路

1. 第一段重点描写图中地球能源即将枯竭这一现实。

2. 第二段从能源保护和人类责任等方面进行解释。

3. 第三段从避免图中所示的严重后果这方面提出个人的观点。

参考范文

What a <u>shocking</u> and thought-provoking scene it is! As is vividly revealed in the drawing above，a man is surprised to find that the oil of our <u>planet</u> is <u>on the verge of</u> <u>exhaustion</u>. What is conveyed in the drawing is realistic and most meaningful.

The implied meaning of the drawing can be interpreted with respect to energy <u>conservation</u> and human responsibility. First of all, it should be recognized that energy conservation is a <u>must</u>. The only source of energy is our planet. Since we only have one planet, it is obvious that our energy including oil is limited. Particularly, the energy of some kinds is not <u>renew-</u>

able. Once it is used up, it is gone for good. What's more, human responsibility obliges us to make wise use of energy instead of using up the energy on our planet. Our predecessors have left a planet rich in natural resources and energy. In the relay of history, how much natural resources and energy will be left to our off-springs is a moral issue. We don't deserve the right to consume the resources and energy which belong to our off-springs. Otherwise, we would strip our off-springs of their survival right. In short, more stress must be laid on energy conservation and human responsibility.

In my view, necessary measures must be taken without any delay so as to avoid the grim status revealed in the drawing. On one hand, a wide campaign should be launched to raise the public's awareness of energy conservation. On the other hand, laws and regulations must be set up in order to punish those who waste energy. Only in these ways can we keep sustainable development and leave a cozy planet to our off-springs.　　　　(286 words)

一句话点评

本文第二段第二点针对能源与道德的论述十分深刻且颇具说服力。

全文翻译

这是多么惊人和发人深省的一幅场景啊！如上图生动所示，一名男子惊讶地发现：我们星球的石油处于枯竭的边缘。本图所传达的信息是真实的并且非常耐人寻味。

本图的深刻含义可以从能源保护和人类责任等方面加以解释。首先，人们应该认识到：能源保护是必须要做的事情。能源的唯一来源是我们的星球。因为我们只有一个星球，显而易见的是我们的能源包括石油是有限的。尤其某些能源是不能再生的。一旦这些不能再生的能源被耗尽，人们就永远地失去了这些能源。此外，人类的责任迫使我们合理地使用能源，而不是耗尽地球上的能源。我们的前辈留给我们一个自然资源和能源丰富的星球。在历史的接力中，我们将把多少自然资源和能源留给我们的后代，这是一个道德问题。我们没有权利去耗费属于我们后代的资源和能源。否则，我们就剥夺了后代生存的权利。总之，我们必须更加强调能源保护和人类责任。

我认为，我们必须立刻采取必要的措施以避免图画中所显示的严峻的情况。一方面，人们应该开展一场广泛的运动来提高公众的能源保护意识。另一方面，我们应该设立法律法规来惩罚那些浪费能源的人。只有以这些方式我们才能保持可持续发展并且留给后代一个舒适的星球。

重点写作词语点睛

shocking	*a.* 令人震惊的	renewable	*a.* 可再生的
planet	*n.* 星球	use up	耗尽
on the verge of...	处于…边缘的	for good	永远
exhaustion	*n.* 耗尽	oblige	*v.* 迫使
conservation	*n.* 保护	predecessor	*n.* 前辈
must	*n.* 必不可少的事	relay	*n.* 接力

natural resources　自然资源　　　　　　status　*n.* 情况，地位

off-springs　后代　　　　　　　　　　cozy　*a.* 舒适的

考研英语短文写作备考试题　　第 38 篇

写作题目与要求

Study the following drawing carefully and write an essay in which you should

1）describe the drawing,

2）interpret the meaning of the drawing, and

3）state your suggestion.

You should write about 160 ～ 200 words neatly on ANSWER SHEET 2. （20 points）

学习不能只为了……　　　　　　　　制图：刘建斌

具体写作思路

1. 第一段对于图画的描述应该突出学生学习的目的。

2. 第二段要围绕目前一些大学生的普遍心态和目前一些大学的教育状况进行论述。

3. 第三段中的建议和措施应该针对第二段所涉及的问题。

参考范文

As is vividly revealed in the drawing above, a student is thinking about money while reading a book. His only purpose of study is to make money. What is indicated in the drawing reflects a fact and is thought-provoking.

The implied meaning of the drawing can be analyzed in terms of students' state of mind and current education on campus. On the one hand, it appears that some students lack a clear orientation of study. Some students are very selfish and self-centred. They only care their own benefits and interests. Making money and self-development are considered as their ultimate goals of study. Their daily study is permeated with money-orientedness. On the other hand, our current education on campus lacks the cultivation of students' spirit and shaping of their soul. Academic work is put on the top of our education agenda. High score is regarded as the most important standard in evaluation of students' development. As a result, some students separate their study with the prosperity of our nation. In one word, we can no longer ignore the students' negative state of mind and the deficiency of our current education.

In my view, some urgent measures must be taken so as to reverse the grim trend reflected in the drawing. To begin with, an education campaign should be launched in order for students to establish a noble objective of study. In addition, government departments at different levels should put more value on the cultivation of students' spirit and soul. Only in these ways can we embrace a promising future of our nation and ensure the healthy development of our society.

(270 words)

一句话点评

本文第二段的论述真实可信且用词得当。

全文翻译

如同图画所逼真地展示，一个学生在读书时考虑着金钱。他学习的唯一目的就是赚钱。图画所暗示的信息反映了一种现实并且发人深省。

图画的含义可以从学生的心态和目前校园教育等方面进行分析。一方面，一些学生似乎缺乏正确的学习目的。一些学生非常自私并且以自我为中心。他们只介意自己的利益。赚钱和自我发展被视为他们学习的唯一目的。他们的日常学习只是向钱看。另外一方面，目前的校园教育缺乏对学生精神的培养和灵魂的塑造。学术工作摆在我们教育日程的首要位置。在学生成长的评价方面，高分被视为最重要的标准。其结果，一些学生把自己的学习和民族的繁荣相分离。总之，我们不能再忽略学生的负面心态以及目前教育的不足。

根据我的观点，一定要采取一些迫切的措施以便扭转目前严峻的趋势。首先，应该展开一场教育运动以便让学生树立高尚的学习目标。另外，不同的政府部门应该重视学生精神和心灵的培养。只有以这些方式，我们才能拥有一个充满希望的民族的未来，并且确保我们社会健康的发展。

重点写作词语点睛

reveal v. 显示	cultivation n. 培养
state of mind 心态	academic a. 学术的
orientation n. 目标；方向	prosperity n. 繁荣
self-centred 自我为中心的	deficiency n. 不足
ultimate a. 最终的	noble a. 高尚的
be permeated with 渗透着	objective n. 目的

考研英语短文写作备考试题   第39篇

写作题目与要求

Study the following pie chart carefully and write an essay in which you should

1) describe the pie chart,
2) define the reason (s) for the support, and
3) give your example.

You should write about 160~200 words neatly on ANSWER SHEET 2. (20 points)

具体写作思路

1. 第一段对于圆饼图的描述应该着重表示支持态度的人群。
2. 第二段的论述要从中国传统文化的角度出发。
3. 第三段中的例子最好涉及中西方文化的两种节日。

参考范文

As is apparently revealed in the pie chart above, the majority people surveyed (62.11%) support the <u>cancellation</u> of May Day long vacation and the establishment of Chinese traditional holidays. What is indicated in the pie chart reflects the pervasive state of mind among average Chinese and is most thought-provoking.

The foremost reasons for the support of the majority can be analyzed with respect to Chinese traditional cultures. To begin with, the establishment of the Chinese traditional holidays is a natural and <u>rational</u> measure. China is an ancient country which has a 5,000-year history. Traditional festivals are the <u>symbol</u> of our Chinese culture. The setting-up of the Chinese traditional holidays is a necessary part of the protection of our national culture and thus should be taken for granted. In addition, the establishment of Chinese traditional holidays indicates our <u>determination</u> to <u>rejuvenate</u> our traditional culture. Over the past years, more and more people in China are westernized and foreign festivals and holidays are gaining favor in China. It seems that we are losing the <u>essence</u> and roots of our own culture. It is a must that we should rescue and rejuvenate Chinese traditional culture. In short, our traditional culture will surely benefit from the new holiday policy.

Take some festivals for example. Over the past years, whenever Christmas comes, most Chinese department stores will extend their business hours till midnight. And young people hold grand Christmas parties and exchange gifts. <u>Relatively speaking</u>, the Spring Festival is getting coolly received. However, it should be realized that a country without its own culture can not establish itself in the world. Therefore, our new holiday policy should be welcomed.

(275 words)

一句话点评

本文第二段的论述有一定的深度剖析且真实可信。

全文翻译

如同圆饼图明确地显示，受调查的大多数人（62.11%）支持取消五一长假并且支持增设中国传统节假日。圆饼图中所暗示的信息反映了普通中国人的心态并且十分发人深省。

大多数人支持的主要原因可以从中国传统文化方面加以分析。首先，增设中国传统文化是自然和理性的措施。中国是一个拥有五千多年历史的古国。传统节日是中国文化的符号。增设中国传统节假日是保护民族文化的必要的一部分，并且应该被认为是理所当然的。此外，增设中国传统节假日显示了我们振兴传统文化的决心。近年来，越来越多的中国人西方化，并且西方节日在中国获得喜爱。我们似乎正在失去自己文化的精髓和根。挽救和振兴中国传统文化是我们应该也是必需要做的事。总之，传统文化必定会从新的节假日政策中获益。

拿一些节日为例。近年来，每当圣诞节来临，大多数中国商店将延长营业时间直到午夜。年轻人举行盛大的圣诞派对并且交流礼物。相对而言，春节正在受到冷遇。然而，应该认识到的是：没有自己文化的国家无法在世界确立自己的地位。因此，我们的新节假日政策应该受到欢迎。

重点写作词语点睛

cancellation	*n.* 取消	rejuvenate	*v.* 振兴
rational	*a.* 理性的	essence	*n.* 精髓
symbol	*n.* 符号	relatively speaking	相对而言
determination	*n.* 决心		

考研英语短文写作备考试题　　第40篇

写作题目与要求

Study the following drawing carefully and write an essay in which you should

1) describe the drawing briefly,

2) explain its intended meaning, and then

3) give your example(s).

You should write about 160 ~ 200 words neatly on ANSWER SHEET 2. (20 points)

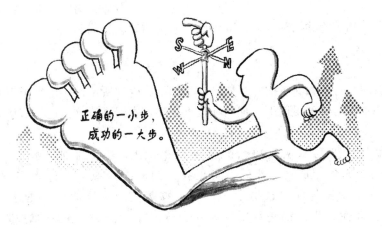

正确的一小步，
成功的一大步。

——正确的一小步　成功的一大步

许英剑/绘画

具体写作思路

1. 第一段重点描写图中男子在指南针的指引下走向成功。
2. 第二段从积累、智慧和细节等方面进行解释。
3. 第三段以邓亚萍为例进行论证。

参考范文

What an interesting and thought-provoking drawing it is! As is vividly revealed in the drawing above, a man is running forward with vigorous strides. Apparently he is approaching success with the help of a compass in his hand. What the drawing intends to convey is most instructive to us, especially young people.

The implied meaning of the drawing can be interpreted in terms of success, accumulation, wisdom and details. First of all, Rome was not built in one day. All people long for success. However, to realize our dream needs a process and accumulation. And nothing could be achieved overnight. Stories of many famous scientists prove that step by step is the only way to success. In addition, every correct and rational step is of importance. As a saying goes "Life is long but its critical point just depends on a few steps". Thus, details of our daily conducts must not be neglected. Whenever a decision needs to be made, we must think before leap. We should make sensible decisions so as to ensure our success. In short, accumulation and rationality should be stressed on our way to success.

Take Deng Yaping for example. She used to be a celebrated table-tennis player. It is her accumulation of relevant skills that has made her realize her Olympic dream. And after she retired, she made a right choice—to learn English in Tsinghua University. It is her practical decision that made her work for the 2008 Beijing Olympic Games successful.　　（248 words）

105

一句话点评

本文第二段的相关论述用词准确，其中的谚语可谓妙笔生花。

全文翻译

这是多么有趣并且发人深省的一幅图画啊！如上图生动所示，一个男子正大步向前跑。显而易见，在其手中指南针的帮助下，他正在接近成功。本图画所欲传达的信息对我们，尤其是年轻人，非常富有教育意义。

本图画的深刻含义可以从成功、积累、智慧和细节等方面加以解释。首先，伟业非一日之功。所有人都渴望成功。然而，实现我们的梦想需要一个过程和积累。任何事情并非一蹴而就。许多著名科学家的事例证明：脚踏实地是通向成功的唯一道路。此外，每一个正确并且理性的步骤都是重要的。常言道："生命虽长但关键处却只有几步。"因此，我们日常行为的细节不能被忽略。每当需要做出决定之前，我们一定要三思而后行。我们需要做出理性的决定以便确保我们的成功。总之，在通往成功的路上，积累和理性应得到重视。

以邓亚萍为例。她曾是一名著名的乒乓球运动员。正是由于相关技能的积累，使她实现了奥运梦想。邓亚萍退役后，做出了一个正确的选择——到清华大学学习英语。恰恰是其切实可行的决定使她为 2008 北京奥运会所做的工作取得成功。

重点写作词语点睛

stride　*n.* 大步	critical　*a.* 重要的
compass　*n.* 指南针	conduct　*n.* 行为
accumulation　*n.* 积累	sensible　*a.* 理智的
detail　*n.* 细节	celebrated　*a.* 著名的
process　*n.* 过程	retire　*v.* 退役
rational　*a.* 合理的	practical　*a.* 切实可行的

考研英语短文写作备考试题　　第 41 篇

写作题目与要求

Study the following drawing carefully and write an essay in which you should

1）describe the drawing,

2）analyze the reasons, and

3）state your suggestion.

You should write about 160 ~ 200 words neatly on ANSWER SHEET 2.（20 points）

具体写作思路

1. 对图中所传达的主要信息进行描述，语言一定要简练。

2. 从以下三方面讨论充电的原因：社会发展的必然；对复合型人才的需求；个人提升和发展的必需。

3. 从完善培训、改善学习环境和法律保护三方面提出自己的建议。

参考范文

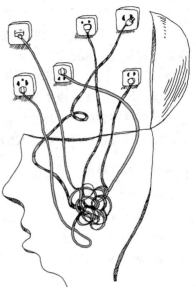

充电计划

摘自《新京报》

As is vividly revealed in the drawing above, a man is busy <u>recharging</u> himself with knowledge, which seems to be humorous but most thought-provoking. At present, such phenomenon is not uncommon in our modern society.

The reasons for the <u>craze</u> of people's recharge with knowledge can be stated as follows. First of all, the development of our society demands recharge. We are living in an era of knowledge <u>explosion</u>. To be exact, if we want to survive in the information era, we have to recharge ourselves with up-to-date knowledge so as to keep up with the pace of our society. What's more, the requirement of our society demands recharge. At present, talents of multi-abilities are most welcome in the job market. As a result, more and more people attempt to pick up the knowledge beyond their majors. Recharge has become a <u>vogue</u>. Last but not least important, personal advancement demands recharge. To get relevant promotion, people must take exams of various kinds and get <u>certificates</u> and <u>diplomas</u>. As a consequence, recharge has become our life-long work. In sum, owing to social and personal factors, recharge has become an <u>indispensable</u> part of our life.

In my view, measures should be taken to encourage the recharge craze. To begin with, systematic and reasonable training should be planned and provided. In addition, more favorable study environment should be created. Last but not least important, relevant laws and regulations must be set up to protect the rights of those who recharge themselves. Only in these ways can we soon <u>embrace</u> the spring of science and a harmonious society.　　(264 words)

一句话点评

本文所论述的充电原因极其真实可信，重点突出，写作思路清晰。

全文翻译

如同上面的图画所生动地显示，一个人正忙于用知识给自己充电，这似乎幽默但却非常发人深省。目前，这种现象在现代社会中是常见的。

人们的知识充电热的原因可以阐述如下。首先，我们社会的发展要求充电。我们生活在一个知识爆炸的时代。准确地讲，如果我们想要在信息时代生存，我们必须用不断更新的知识来对自己充电以便跟上社会的步伐。此外，我们社会的要求需要人们充电。目前，复合型人才在就业市场中最受欢迎。结果，越来越多的人努力学会其专业以外的知识。充电已经成为一种时尚。最后但并非最不重要的一点，个人的发展要求充电。为了得到相应的发展，人们必须参加各类考试并且得到证书和文凭。结果，充电已经成为我们一生的工作。总之，由于社会和个人的因素，充电已经成为我们生活中不可缺少的一部分。

我认为，应该采取措施鼓励充电热。首先，应当规划和提供系统的和合理的培训。此外，应该创造更有利的学习环境。最后但并非最不重要的一点，一定要制定相应法规来保护充电人的权益。只有以这种方法，我们才能在不久的将来拥抱科学的春天和和谐的社会。

重点写作词语点睛

recharge *v.* 充电
certificate *n.* 证书

craze *n.* 热
diploma *n.* 文凭

explosion *n.* 爆炸
indispensable *a.* 不可缺少的

vogue *n.* 时尚
embrace *v.* 拥抱

考研英语短文写作备考试题　　第 42 篇

写作题目与要求

Study the following drawing carefully and write an essay in which you should

1）describe the drawing,

2）interpret the purpose of the painter, and

3）give your example.

You should write about 160～200 words neatly on ANSWER SHEET 2.（20 points）

具体写作思路

1. 第一段对图画的描述应该针对图中男子的不文明行为。
2. 第二段的论述应该从讲文明和树新风方面展开。
3. 第三段的实例最好是众所周知的游客不文明行为。

参考范文

As is vividly revealed in the drawing above, a visitor is standing on the top of a cultural relic to have a picture taken. He is proud of his own action. What is conveyed in the drawing reflects a common social phenomenon in public places and is most thought-provoking.

The main purpose of the painter can be interpreted in terms of stressing civilization and setting up a new trend. To begin with, stressing civilization is badly needed in public places. At present, some people ignore civilization and perform misconducts of various kinds. It is not uncommon that some people jump the line, spitting on the ground, littering waste and speaking loudly in public places. All the bad manners do harm to the creation of our harmonious society. In addition, setting-up a new trend is also necessary in the development of a modern society. It is no doubt that our living standard has been greatly improved. But we should not neglect the development of our spiritual civilization. As a modern citizen, we should display a higher level of morality. In short, stressing civilization and setting up a new trend should be put on our agenda.

Take some tourists for example. Some Chinese visitors to western countries shout loudly at dinner tables. Others force foreigners to have a picture taken. Still others spoil the lawn. All these uncivilized conducts have damaged the international image of P. R. China. The campaign of stressing civilization and setting-up a new trend should be launched so as to protect our international image and build up a harmonious society. (262 words)

一句话点评

本文第三段所列举的典型实例恰到好处。

全文翻译

如图画逼真地显示，一名游客站在一个历史文物的上面拍照。他甚至为自己的行为感到骄傲。图画所传达的内容反映了一种常见的社会现象并且十分发人深省。

图画作者的主要目的可以从讲文明树新风方面加以解释。首先，在建立和谐社会中需要文明。目前，一些人忽略文明并且做出各种不当行为。常见的是：一些人不排队、随地吐痰、乱扔废物并且在公众场合大声喧哗。所有的这些行为损害了和谐社会的建设。此外，在现代社会发展中树新风也是必要的。毫无疑问的是我们的生活水平大大地提高了。但是，我们不应该忽略精神文明的发展。作为现代公民，我们应该显示更高的道德水平。总之，讲文明树新风应该提到我们的议事日程上来。

拿一些中国游客为例。一些去西方国家的游客在就餐时大声喧哗。另一些游客强迫外国人拍照。还有一些游客破坏草坪。所有这些不文明行为损害了中国的国际形象。应该掀起一场讲文明树新风的运动以便保护我们的国际形象并且建设一个和谐社会。

重点写作词语点睛

cultural relic　文物

civilization　*n.* 文明

misconduct　*n.* 不当行为

standard　*n.* 水平

morality　*n.* 道德

agenda　*n.* 议事日程

spoil　*v.* 破坏

image　*n.* 形象

考研英语短文写作备考试题　　第 43 篇

写作题目与要求

Study the following drawing carefully and write an essay in which you should

1）describe the drawing,

2）analyze the meaning, and

3）give an example.

You should write about 160 ~ 200 words neatly on ANSWER SHEET 2.（20 points）

具体写作思路

1. 对图中所传递的重要信息进行描述，要重点突出。

2. 从以下两方面讨论本图的含义：学生过分重视专业的选择及其不良后果；学生选专业时应因人而异。

3. 用个人的例子来说明问题。

参考范文

　　As is vividly demonstrated in the drawing above, facing so many major <u>options</u>, a student is at a complete loss what to do, which is a most typical phenomenon among students. The meaning conveyed in the drawing is most thought-provoking.

　　The implied meaning of the drawing above can be briefly stated as follows. To begin with, the <u>over-emphasis</u> of importance of <u>majors</u> by students should not be ignored. Some students <u>reckon</u> that their majors will decide the success or failure of their whole lives. Because of their dissatisfaction with their majors, some students lose their

摘自《新京报》2005 年 4 月 25 日

interest in study. And some of them even go extreme and commit suicide. It is our top priority to reverse the grim situation. What's more, in terms of making major choices, to follow suit must be avoided. As we know, different people are needed to play different roles in our social work. It is out of the question that all the people pick up the same major and do the same work. Personal character, interest, and merit must be fully evaluated and seriously considered when students make their final decision on their majors. In sum, students must keep calm and have an objective attitude toward their majors.

Take myself as an example. I am from a small mountainous village from the West. The ambition has already taken roots in my mind that I will make use of my knowledge to help the farmers in my home-village shake off poverty. And I took an interest in plants when I was a child. All things considered, I chose agronomy as my major. I do reckon that I have a bright prospect if I stick to the major I choose.　　　　　　　　　　　　　　　　　　　（282 words）

一句话点评

本文的论述极其客观和真实，最后一段的例子非常贴切，全文用词准确。

全文翻译

如同上面的图画所生动地显示一样，一名学生面对过多的专业选择感到茫然而不知所措，这是学生中一种非常典型的现象。这幅图画所传达的含义非常发人深省。

上面图画所传递的含义可以简述如下。首先，不应该忽略学生对于专业重要性的过分重视的现象。一些学生认为他们的专业将决定其整个人生的成功或失败。由于他们对专业的不满，一些学生丧失对学习的兴趣。其中的一些学生甚至走向极端以致自杀。扭转这种严峻的状况是我们的当务之急。此外，就进行专业选择而言，一定要避免从众行为。我们知道，我们的社会需要不同的人在工作中扮演不同的角色。所有的人都选择同样的专业并做同样的工作是不可能的。当学生做出有关其专业的最终决定时，一定要充分评估和认真考虑个人性格、兴趣和优点。总之，学生一定要保持冷静并且拥有一个客观的态度对待自己的专业。

以我自己为例，我来自于西部的一个小山村。充分利用我的知识来帮助家乡的农民脱贫的志向在我心中已经扎根。当我是个孩子的时候，我就对植物有兴趣。考虑到这一切，我选择农学作为我的专业。我的确认为如果我坚持我选择的专业，我就会有一个光明的未来。

重点写作词语点睛

option　*n.* 选择	go extreme　走向极端
over-emphasis　过分强调	follow suit　跟着做，照着做
major　*n.* 专业	attitude　*n.* 态度
reckon　*v.* 认为	shake off poverty　脱贫

写作题目与要求

Study the following drawing carefully and write an essay in which you should

1）describe the drawing briefly,

2）explain the intended purpose of the painter, and then

3）give your example(s).

You should write about 160 ~ 200 words neatly on ANSWER SHEET 2.（20 points）

——考验冠军

路易斯/绘画

具体写作思路

1. 第一段重点描写图中 3 个人的不同境况与心态。

2. 第二段从辛勤的努力和独一无二的能力等方面进行解释。

3. 第三段以邓亚萍为例进行论证。

参考范文

What a humorous and thought-provoking scene it is! As is vividly revealed in the drawing above, a man is looking up at the champion <u>platform</u> while two other men are merrily standing on the platforms for <u>runner-up</u> and the third place winner. The platform for the gold medalist is so high that the man is somewhat afraid. What is conveyed in the drawing is most meaningful to all of us.

The purpose of the painter can be interpreted with respect to painstaking efforts and unique capability. First of all, "No pains, no gains." We all want to be champions and excel others in life, work and study. However, only by painstaking efforts can we make our ideal come true. Champions need to make greater painstaking efforts, endure more hardships and overcome more difficulties. What's more, wisdom is also a must so as for us to become champions. The path to success is longer and rugged. We must constantly sum up our frustrations and failures so that we can be equipped with unique conviction and relevant skills. Otherwise, we cannot remove obstacles and win the race. In sum, the growth of a champion cannot be separated with sweat, persistence and wisdom.

Take Deng Yaping for example. She is physically at disadvantage to be a table-tennis player due to her height. But she did not retreat. It is her years of sweat, tears, persistence and wisdom in training and competition that have paved her way to be a great Olympic champion.

(249 words)

一句话点评

本文第三段所选用的邓亚萍事例十分贴题且颇具说服力。

全文翻译

这是多么幽默且发人深省的一幅场景啊！如同上图生动所示，一名男子正在抬头仰望冠军领奖台，而此时另外两名男子正在愉快地站在亚军和季军的领奖台上。冠军的领奖台太高了以至于这名男子有点儿害怕。本图所传达的信息对于我们大家均意味深长。

本图作者的目的可以从辛勤的努力和独一无二的能力等方面加以解释。首先，"没有付出就没有收获"。我们都想成为冠军并且在生活、工作和学习方面超过别人。但是，只有通过辛勤的努力，我们才能使理想成为现实。冠军需要做出更大的努力、忍受更多的困苦并且克服更多的困难。此外，我们成为冠军，智慧也是一个必需的要素。通往成功的道路更长并且崎岖。我们必须不断地总结挫折和失败以便用独一无二的信念和相应的技能武装自己。否则，我们无法消除障碍并赢得比赛。总之，冠军的成长与汗水、坚持和智慧是不可分离的。

以邓亚萍为例。由于身高因素，邓亚萍在身体条件方面处于劣势。但是她没有放弃。恰恰是邓亚萍多年来在训练和比赛中的汗水、泪水、坚持和智慧为她成为伟大的奥运冠军铺平了道路。

重点写作词语点睛

platform *n.* 平台	endure *v.* 忍受
runner-up 亚军	wisdom *n.* 明智；智慧
painstaking *a.* 辛勤的	rugged *a.* 崎岖的
unique *a.* 独一无二的	frustration *n.* 挫折
excel *v.* 超过	be equipped with… 用…武装
come true 实现	conviction *n.* 信念

remove *v.* 消除   retreat *v.* 退却

disadvantage *n.* 劣势   pave one's way 铺平道路

考研英语短文写作备考试题　　第 45 篇

写作题目与要求

Study the following drawing carefully and write an essay in which you should

1) describe the drawing briefly,

2) analyze the intended purpose of the painter, and then

3) give your example(s).

You should write about 160~200 words neatly on ANSWER SHEET 2. (20 points)

——总结

夏明/绘画

具体写作思路

1. 第一段重点描写图中左侧的人以及其手中的完美无缺苹果的图片。
2. 第二段从态度、客观和诚实等方面进行相关分析。
3. 第三段以中国乒乓球队为例进行论证。

参考范文

What a <u>typical</u> and thought-provoking scene it is. As is vividly demonstrated in the drawing above, a man is showing a photo of a <u>perfect</u> apple to a photographer, indicating that the latter should not make an imperfect <u>summing-up</u> of him. The apples in the picture are <u>impressive</u>. What is conveyed in the drawing is both instructive and meaningful.

The purpose of the painter can be briefly analyzed in terms of attitude, <u>objectivity</u> and <u>integrity</u>. To begin with, it is necessary for us to "Call a spade a spade." Since our intention to sum up is to improve our work and study, it is <u>imperative</u> that we <u>possess</u> adequate courage to admit the reality and face our defects. Otherwise, our summing-up efforts are <u>futile</u>. What's more, it should be recognized that "To err is human." As a social being, we have both <u>merits</u> and <u>shortcomings</u>. It is inevitable for us to make mistakes now and then. However, making mistakes is not <u>horrible</u>. To sum up our defects and <u>modestly</u> accept others' criticism is most <u>critical</u> to our self-development because by doing so we can avoid making the same mistake in the future. In short, the right attitude and courage to face our defects and modest acceptance of others' <u>criticism</u> can benefit our life, work and study.

Take Chinese Table-tennis Team for example. The team has won numerous gold medals in international sports events and is the <u>pride</u> of our nation. However, it is hardly known that it is its <u>regular</u> objective and realistic summing-up of its <u>advantages</u> and disadvantages that keeps the very team moving on. The team has set us a good example and we should learn from it.

(280 words)

一句话点评

本文第一段针对图画信息内容进行了合理地归纳和总结。

全文翻译

这是多么典型且发人深省的一幅场景啊！如上图所生动地展示，一个男子正在向一名摄影师出示一张完美苹果的照片，暗示摄影师不应该给他一份不完美的总结。图片中的苹果给人留下了深刻的印象。本图所传达的信息既有教育意义又耐人寻味。

本图作者的目的可以从态度、客观和诚实等方面进行简单的分析。首先，"实事求是"是必要的。因为我们总结的意图是改进我们的工作和学习，所以，我们必须拥有足够的勇气去承认现实并且面对缺点。否则，我们的总结是无益的。此外，我们应该认识到：人生在世，孰能无错。作为社会中的人，我们既有优点又有缺点。我们时不时地犯错误是不可避免的。但是，犯错误并不可怕。总结我们的不足并且谦虚地接受别人的批评对我们的自我发展是非常重要的，因为这样做我们可以避免在未来犯同样的错误。总之，面对我们缺点的正确态度和勇气以及虚心接受别人的批评能使我们的生活、工作和学习获益。

以中国乒乓球队为例。该队在国际体育赛事中获得了无数金牌并且是我们民族的骄傲。但是，鲜为人知的是：恰恰是该队对自身优势和劣势的定期、客观的且真实的总结使该队不断前进。该队为我们树立了好的榜样，我们应该向中国乒乓球队学习。

重点写作词语点睛

typical   *a.* 典型的   perfect   *a.* 完美的

the latter 后者

summing-up 总结

impressive *a.* 留下深刻印象的

objectivity *n.* 客观

integrity *n.* 诚实

imperative *u.* 迫切的，必要的

possess *v.* 具有

futile *a.* 无效的

merit *n.* 优点

shortcoming *n.* 缺点

horrible *a.* 可怕的

modestly *ad.* 谦虚地

critical *a.* 重要的

criticism *n.* 批评

pride *n.* 骄傲

regular *a.* 定期的

advantage *n.* 优势

考研英语短文写作备考试题　　第 46 篇

写作题目与要求

Study the following drawing carefully and write an essay in which you should

1）describe the drawing，

2）deduce the purpose of the painter and

3）suggest counter-measures.

You should write about 160 ~ 200 words neatly on ANSWER SHEET 2.（20 points）

［观棋不语］

摘自《长江日报》2004 年 11 月 18 日

具体写作思路

1. 对图中所传达的重要信息进行措施，并指出其重要性。

2. 从是非观念出发利用公共汽车上的偷窃案件对本图的目的进行讨论。

3. 从提高公众觉悟和立法两个方面提出应对措施。

参考范文

As is vividly betrayed in the drawing above, the people who are watching the chess game are reluctant to openly express their opinions about what is right and what is wrong though they can tell the right from the wrong. The drawing is really thought-provoking.

The aim of the painter of the drawing is to reveal the fact that people in modern society are losing the courage to openly support what is right and condemn what is wrong due to their personal interests. The theft case in the bus is a case in point. Most often, nobody is brave enough to stop the thief. Sometimes the person who stops the thief in the bus is seriously injured by the thief with other passengers doing nothing to help on the spot. It is quite common that some victims dare not admit in public that their properties are stolen. Such cases are increasing and threatening our society.

Counter-measures should be taken to avoid the cases mentioned above. To begin with, we must launch a campaign to popularize the world outlook of sticking to what is right and condemning what is wrong. What's more, we must establish relevant laws to award those who support what is right and punish those who avoid and escape when they are encountering the wrong.

(217 words)

一句话点评

准确的语言、清晰的思路、恰当的例子是本文的特点。

全文翻译

如同上面的图画所形象地显示一样，观看象棋比赛的人不愿意公开表达自己有关是非的意见，尽管他们能够区分是与非。这幅图画的确令人深省。

图画作者的目的是要揭示一个事实：出于个人利益考虑，现代社会中的人们正在丧失公开支持"是"和公开谴责"非"的勇气。公共汽车上的偷窃案件就是一个例子。通常，没有人足以勇敢地站出来制止小偷。有时，在公共汽车上制止小偷的人被小偷严重伤害，而其他乘客却在现场无动于衷。常见的是一些受害者不敢公开承认他们的财产被盗。类似事件日益增长并且威胁我们的社会。

应该采取应对措施以避免上面所提到的情况。首先，我们必须发起一次运动来普及坚持"是"和谴责"非"的世界观。此外，我们一定要确立相应的法律来奖励那些支持"是"的人，惩罚那些面对"非"时回避和逃脱的人。

重点写作词语点睛

be reluctant to 不愿意	on the spot 在现场
tell *v.* 区分	property *n.* 财产
thought-provoking 发人深省的	threaten *v.* 威胁
condemn *v.* 谴责	stick to 坚持

写作题目与要求

Study the following drawing carefully and write an essay in which you should

1）describe the drawing,

2）interpret its meaning, and

3）suggest counter-measures.

You should write about 160 ~ 200 words neatly on AN-SWER SHEET 2.（20 points）

具体写作思路

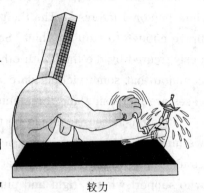

较力

（绘画：黎青）

1. 对图中所传递的重要信息进行描述，并指出对中国的重要性。

2. 从以下两个方面讨论本图的含义：现代发展与保护传统建筑之间的关系；保护传统建筑与尊重传统文化的关系。

3. 从立法和提高公众意识两个方面提出应对措施。

参考范文

As is vividly betrayed in the drawing above, a huge modern high-rise building is contesting with a small and ancient pavilion, which mirrors a common social phenomenon that our ancient and traditional architectures are gradually replaced with high-rise architectures made of steel and cement. In a country of over-5 000-year history, the current situation is indeed thought-provoking.

The implied meaning of the drawing above can be illustrated as follows. To begin with, the protection of ancient and traditional architectures should not be neglected in the development of our modern society. In the evolution of a society, the construction of high-rise buildings are necessary, but only rational construction of new buildings and discreet protection of ancient and traditional architectures can make a city preserve its vitality. through In one word, a city which is of both unique traditional characteristics and modern features can finally survive and be inviting in the world. What's more, to protect the ancient and traditional architectures means that we show respect to our culture and history. As a Chinese, we should have a better understanding of the importance of culture, history and tradition. In the development of our society, we should also take into consideration how to hand down our cultural heritages to our next generations. Otherwise, we will commit historical mistakes.

Counter-measures must be taken immediately so as to curb the destruction of valuable ancient and traditional architectures. Most importantly, relevant laws and regulations must be established to protect the valuable architectures. Besides, we must spare no efforts to popularize the importance of the protection work.

(272 words)

一句话点评

本文抓住了图中所要表达的主题——保护有价值的传统建筑，并且在论述中用词生动贴切。

全文翻译

如同上面的图画所生动地显示一样，一幢巨大的现代高层建筑正在和一个小小的、古老的凉亭较力。这反映了一种常见的社会现象：我们的古老和传统建筑正逐渐地被由钢筋和水泥构成的高层建筑所取代。在一个拥有 5 000 多年历史的国家，当前的形势的确发人深省。

上面图画所传达的含义可以阐述如下。首先，在现代社会的发展中不应该忽略古老和传统建筑的保护。在社会发展中高层建筑是必需的，但是只有合理建设新建筑并且合理保护古老和传统建筑，才能使城市保持其活力。一句话，既具有独特传统特色又具有现代特点的城市才能最终在世界上存在并且具有吸引力。其次，保护古老和传统的建筑意味着我们尊重自己的文化和历史。作为中国人，我们应该对文化、历史和传统的重要性有着更深刻的理解。在社会发展中，我们还应该考虑如何把我们的文化遗产传给下一代。否则，我们将犯历史性的错误。

应该立即采取应对措施以便阻止对于有价值的古老和传统建筑的破坏。非常重要的是，一定要制定相关法规以便保护有价值的建筑。此外，我们一定要不遗余力地普及保护工作的重要性。

重点写作词语点睛

high-rise building　高层建筑物	preserve　*v.* 保存
pavilion　*n.* 亭子	vitality　*n.* 活力
architecture　*n.* 建筑	consideration　*n.* 因素
rational　*a.* 理性的	hand down　传递

考研英语短文写作备考试题　　第48篇

写作题目与要求

Study the following drawing carefully and write an essay in which you should

1）describe the drawing,

2）interpret its meaning, and

3）suggest counter-measures.

You should write about 160 ~ 200 words neatly on ANSWER SHEET 2. (20 points)

摘自《北京晨报》2004 年 5 月 24 日

具体写作思路

1. 对图中所传达的重要信息进行描述，并指出其重要性。

2. 从以下两个方面讨论本图的含义：学生需要良好的心理素质；学生需要较高的道德水平。

3. 从人们所应具备的正确态度和加强政府的干预两方面提出应对措施。

参考范文

As is vividly betrayed in the drawing above, a student is trying his best to reach the full score of his important subjects including English, maths, physics, and Chinese while neglecting his more important aspects such as psychological quality and moral standards. This drawing mirrors a common social phenomenon, which should arouse our social concern.

The implied meaning of the drawing above can be illustrated as follows. To begin with, academic achievements are not all that a student most needs. In order to survive in our society, students must be first of all trained to possess fine psychological quality. Otherwise, we can not bravely face ups and downs in our life, work and study. What's more, high moral standards are also a must for every student. Without high moral standards, students will lose the orientation of learning. Most often, even though a student possesses profound academic knowledge, he can not find himself a right place in our society and this is unable to make contribution to his motherland due to his low moral standards. It is often reported in our daily newspapers that university undergraduates and graduate commit crimes. Ma Jiajue, a student in Yunnan University, is a case in point. In sum, psychological quality and moral standards should be taken into account in terms of students' education.

Counter-measures must be taken immediately so as to reverse the trend revealed in the drawing. First of all, we must take a right attitude toward students' development. What's more, government departments at different levels must intervene in students' education to ensure a right and healthy environment of development.

(266 words)

一句话点评

本文对图画中所隐藏的信息进行了深刻的剖析，文中的例子十分具有说服力。

全文翻译

如同上面的图画所生动地显示一样，一名学生正全力以赴去争取其包括英语、数学、物理和中文在内主要科目的满分，与此同时他忽略了心理素质和道德水平等更重要的方面。本图反映了一个常见的社会现象，应该引起社会的关注。

上面图画所表达的含义可以阐述如下。首先，学术成绩并非学生最需要的一切。为了在社会中生存，学生应该首先被培训以便具有良好的心理素质。否则，我们无法勇敢地面对生活、工作和学习中的起伏。没有较高的道德标准，学生们将丧失学习的目的和方向。通常，即使一名学生具有渊博的学术知识，由于其较低的道德水平，他也无法在社会中寻找到自己合适的位置，因此无法为祖国作出贡献。报纸上经常报道大学在校生和毕业生犯罪。云南大学学生马加爵就是一个例子。总之，就学生的教育而言，应该考虑心理素质和道德水平。

应该立即采取应对措施以便扭转图中所显示的趋势。首先，我们对学生的成长一定要采取一个正确的态度。其次，各级政府部门一定要干预学生的教育以便确保一个合适和健康的成长环境。

重点写作词语点睛

subject n. 科目	possess v. 具有
psychological quality 心理素质	orientation n. 目的，方向
academic achievement 学术成就	profound a. 深厚的
moral standard 道德标准	undergraduate n. 本科生

考研英语短文写作备考试题　　第 49 篇

写作题目与要求

Study the following drawing carefully and write an essay in which you should

1）describe the drawing,

2）interpret its meaning, and

3) state your suggestion.

You should write about 160~200 words neatly on ANSWER SHEET 2. （20 points）

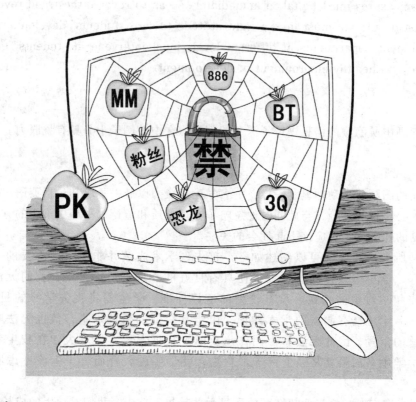

具体写作思路

1. 对图中所传达的重要信息进行描述，并指出网络语言问题的重要性。

2. 从以下两方面讨论本图的含义：网络语言应该引起人们的注意；对网络语言应该持客观的态度。

3. 从客观态度和呼吁停止创造荒诞离奇的网络词语两个方面提出自己的建议。

参考范文

As is vividly revealed in the drawing above, network language has been <u>coined</u> with the emergence of computer and some people are holding <u>negative</u> attitude towards network language. At present, network language has become a social issue and is indeed worth discussing among the general public.

The implied meaning of the drawing can be briefly stated as follows. To begin with, it is high time that we <u>took into account</u> network language. Over the past years, with the popularity of computers and the availability of internet, network language has undergone a <u>robust</u> development and as a result network language has become a <u>vogue</u> among young people. At present, <u>due</u> attention should be paid to the increasing popularity of network language.

What's more, it is necessary for us to avoid the use of some network language. For the time being, some network language are ridiculous and far-fetched. For instance, "886" is employed to express "Bye Bye" and "3Q" to express "Thank you". The existence of such network language is bound to spoil both Chinese and English. Therefore, we had better forbid network language of the kind. In sum, the issue of network language should be put on the top of our agenda.

In my view, some necessary measures should be taken to ensure a healthy development of network language. On the one hand, people should maintain an objective attitude towards the emergence of network language. On the other hand, netizens had better stop creating ridiculous and far-fetched network words and phrases. Only in these ways can we have a harmonious network environment and charming languages.

(265 words)

一句话点评

本文围绕关注网络语言和对网络语言应持有客观态度两个方面对一个比较热门的话题进行了生动的论述，用词十分准确。

全文翻译

如同上面的图画所逼真地揭示的一样，由于电脑的出现网络语言被创造出来。一些人对网络语言持否定的态度。目前网络语言已经成为一个社会问题并且的确值得在公众中展开讨论。

上面图画的深层含义可以被简述如下。首先，我们该考虑网络语言了。近年来，由于电脑和互联网的普及，网络语言经历了迅猛的发展，其结果导致网络语言在年轻人中成为一种时尚。目前，应该给予网络语言应有的注意。此外，必要的是我们应该避免使用某些网络语言。现在，一些网络语言荒谬且牵强。例如："886"用来表达英语的"Bye-bye"，"3Q"用来表达英语的"Thank you"。这类网络语言的存在注定有损于中文和英文。因此，我们最好禁止这类网络语言。总之，网络语言的问题应该放到我们的议事日程之首。

根据我的观点，应该采取一些必要的措施来确保网络语言的健康发展。一方面，人们应该对网络语言的出现保持一个客观的态度。另一方面，网名最好停止创造荒谬和牵强的网络词语。只有以上述方式我们才会拥有一个和谐的网络环境以及具有魅力的语言。

重点写作词语点睛

coin v. 创造	due a. 应有的
negative a. 消极的	far-fetched 牵强的
take into account 考虑	forbid v. 禁止
robust a. 有活力的	emergence n. 出现
vogue n. 时尚	netizen n. 网民

写作题目与要求

Study the following photo carefully and write an essay in which you should

1）describe the photo,

2）interpret the meaning of the drawing, and

3）give your example.

You should write about 160 ~ 200 words neatly on ANSWER SHEET 2.（20 points）

具体写作思路

1. 第一段对于图片的描述应该着重于队员们的同舟共济。

2. 第二段的论述要围绕合作意识和团队精神来展开。

3. 第三段中的例子应该是最鲜活且有说服力的实例。

参考范文

As is vividly betrayed in the photo above, four people are making joint efforts in a boat race. All of them cooperate and spare no effort to win success. What is indicated in the picture above reflects a common sense and is most thought-provoking.

The implied meaning of the picture above can be interpreted in terms of cooperation and teamwork. To begin with, the sense of cooperation must be cultivated among us. As social beings, people depend on each other in our daily life, work and study. The realization of self-value is closely related to unity and cooperation. It is well-known that "United we stand, divided we fall". What's more, the spirit of cooperation and teamwork is badly needed in the building-up of a harmonious society. As we know, the social development is based on the contribution and cooperation of every citizen. The spirit of cooperation and teamwork benefits both our social harmony and each individual. And sincere cooperation will surely bring us the prosperity of a nation. In short, it is essential for us to be aware of the importance of cooperation and teamwork.

Take Shenzhou and Chang'e space-crafts for example. Both of the projects are demanding tasks. The research and experiment work is permeated with the spirit of cooperation and sacrifice. Without such cooperation and sacrifice, the success of the two space-crafts would not be achieved. In sum, the sense of cooperation and teamwork should take roots in our minds.

(241 words)

一句话点评

本文第三段所列举的实例颇具说服力。

全文翻译

如同图片所生动地显示,四个人正在共同努力进行划船比赛。他们相互合作不遗余力地去赢得比赛的胜利。图片所暗示的信息反映了一个常识并且十分发人深省。

图片的含义可以从合作和团队精神等方面加以解释。首先,一定要在我们当中培养合作意识。作为社会中的人,人们在日常生活、工作以及学习中彼此相互依赖。个人价值的实现与团结和合作密切相关。众所周知:"联合,我们就生存;分裂,我们就灭亡。"此外,在建设和谐社会中迫切需要合作和团队精神。正如我们所知,社会发展基于每个公民的贡献和合作。合作和团队精神既有利于我们的社会又有益于每个人。真诚的合作必将为我们带来一个民族的繁荣。总之,重要的是我们要知道合作和团队精神的重要性。

举神州和嫦娥太空飞船为例。这两个项目都是艰巨的任务。研究和实验工作充满合作和牺牲的精神。没有这样的合作和牺牲,这两个太空飞船的成功就无法取得。总之,合作和团队的意识应该在我们心中扎根。

重点写作词语点睛

betray	v. 显示	self-value	自我价值
common sense	常识	prosperity	n. 繁荣
cooperation	n. 合作	space-craft	太空飞船
teamwork	n. 团队精神	demanding	a. 艰巨的
cultivate	v. 培养	sacrifice	n. 牺牲

第三部分 考研英语应用文写作
备考试题 (1~50篇)

考研英语应用文写作备考试题   第1篇

写作题目与要求

At present, much attention is being attached to the environmental protection. Write a letter to advocate car-pooling. And in your letter, you should at least state the aim of your writing and the advantage(s) of car-pooling.

You should write about 100 words on ANSWER SHEET 2. Do not sign your own name at the end of the letter. Use "Li Ming" instead. You do not need to write the address. (10 points)

具体写作思路

1. 以一名学生的身份介绍自己并说明写此信的目的。
2. 说明拼车的益处。
3. 感谢大家的配合。

参考范文

A Letter of Advocacy (Appeal)

Jan. 15, 2011

Dear Sir or Madam,

I, the undersigned, am an ordinary student of Beijing University of Science and Technology. As a volunteer of environmental protection, I am writing to recommend car-pooling to you.

At present, car-pooling has many advantages. In terms of environmental protection, car-pooling reduces waste-gas emission and air pollution. Besides, car-pooling helps cut down the energy consumption. Most importantly, car-pooling can ease traffic pressure and lower our transportation fee. All these help promote the harmony between human beings and nature.

Let's make joint efforts to create a green and harmonious environment. Your cooperation would be much appreciated.

Sincerely yours,

Li Ming

(105 words)

一句话点评

本文第二段有关拼车所带来的相关益处的阐述具体翔实并且言之有物。

全文翻译

一封倡议书

亲爱的女士们、先生们：

  我，下面签名的人，是北京科学与技术大学的一名普通的学生。作为一名环保志愿者，我写此信提倡大家拼车。

  目前，拼车有许多益处。就环境保护而言，拼车减少废气的排放和空气污染。此外，拼车有助于减少能源消耗。非常重要的是：拼车能够缓解交通压力并且降低交通费用。所有这一切有助于促进人与自然的和谐。

  让我们为创建一个绿色和和谐的环境做出共同的努力。感谢你的合作。

真诚的

李明

2011 年 1 月 15 日

重点写作词语点睛

environmental protection	环境保护	recommend *v.*	推荐
car-pooling	拼车	advantage *n.*	好处；优势
emission *n.*	排放	consumption *n.*	消耗
ease *v.*	缓解	harmonious *a.*	和谐的

考研英语应用文写作备考试题　第 2 篇

写作题目与要求

As a social worker and a volunteer, write a letter to all citizens in Beijing to ask them to smile.

You should write about 100 words on ANSWER SHEET 2. Do not sign your own name at the end of the letter. Use "Li Ming" instead. You do not need to write the address. (10 points)

具体写作思路

1. 首先介绍自己并说出写此信的目的。
2. 说明微笑的重要性。

A Letter of Advocacy

Jan. 15, 2011

To Every Citizen,

　　I, the undersigned, am a senior in Tsinghua University and also a social worker and a volunteer. I am writing to advocate all citizens in Beijing to smile.

　　China is a country with the most friendly people. Smile is the most sincere invitation that we send to the friends all over the world. China is also a country with 5 000-year history and civilization. Smile is the best representation of our culture and etiquette. Besides, China is a country which is developing rapidly. Smile is our great confidence that China will be more prosperous.

　　Therefore, let's smile. Give the world the sweetest smile!

Sincerely yours,

Li Ming

(122 words)

一句话点评

　　本文第二段针对微笑的必要性的解释和说明真实、具体并且十分有说服力。

全文翻译

一封倡议书

致每位公民：

　　我，下面签名的人，是清华大学一名大四的学生，也是一名社会工作者和志愿者。我写信倡导所有北京的公民微笑。

　　中国是一个拥有最友好人民的国家。微笑是我们向全世界的朋友发出的最真诚的邀请。中国还是一个拥有五千年历史和文明的国家。微笑是我们文化和礼仪的最佳体现。除此之外，中国是一个发展迅速的国家。微笑是我们的自信：中国将更加繁荣。

　　因此，让我们微笑。给世界最甜美的微笑。

你忠诚的

李明

2011 年 1 月 15 日

重点写作词语点睛

advocacy   *n.* 倡议   social worker   社会工作者

volunteer   *n.* 志愿者   advocate   *v.* 倡议

invitation   *n.* 邀请   civilization   *n.* 文明

representation   *n.* 体现   etiquette   *n.* 礼仪

confidence   *n.* 自信

考研英语应用文写作备考试题　第3篇

写作题目与要求

As 2012 London Olympic Games is drawing near, write a letter to all Chinese spectators to ask them to watch sports matches in a civilized manner.

You should write about 100 words on ANSWER SHEET 2. Do not sign your own name at the end of the letter. Use "Li Ming" instead. You do not need to write the address. (10 points)

具体写作思路

1. 首先介绍自己并说出写此信的目的。
2. 说明文明观看比赛的重要性。

参考范文

A Letter of Advocacy

Jan. 15, 2011

To Every Chinese Spectator,

　　I, the undersigned, am a senior in Peking University. I am writing the letter to advocate all the Chinese audience to watch sports events in a civilized manner.

　　China is a nation of 5 000-year history and civilization. Watching sports matches in a civilized manner is the representation of our culture and etiquette. Olympic Games is a window through which we introduce China to the world. Uncivilized conducts not only spoil the international image of China but also disturb the normal order of sports events. Sometimes such misconducts may hinder the performance of most athletes and prevents the healthy development of sports.

　　Therefore, let's take immediate action so as to prepare for watching 2012 London

Olympic Games in a civilized manner.

Sincerely yours,

Li Ming

（134 words）

一句话点评

本文第二段对做文明观众意义的阐述真实具体。

全文翻译

一封倡议信

致每位中国观众：

我，下面签名的人，是北京大学一名大四的学生。我写信倡导所有的中国观众文明观看比赛。

中国是一个具有五千年历史和文明的国家。文明观看体育比赛是我们文化和礼仪的体现。奥运会是一个窗口，通过这个窗口我们把中国介绍给世界。不文明的行为不仅破坏中国的国际形象而且扰乱体育比赛的正常秩序。有时不文明的行为还会妨碍大多数运动员的发挥甚至阻碍体育的健康发展。

因此，让我们立即采取措施以便为文明观看伦敦 2012 年奥运会做准备。

真诚的

李明

2011 年 1 月 15 日

重点写作词语点睛

spectator	*n.* 观众	audience	*n.* 观众
civilized	*a.* 文明的	representation	*n.* 体现
etiquette	*n.* 礼仪	uncivilized	*a.* 不文明的
conduct	*n.* 行为	spoil	*v.* 损害
disturb	*v.* 扰乱	order	*n.* 秩序
performance	*n.* 表现	healthy	*a.* 健康的

考研英语应用文写作备考试题　第 4 篇

写作题目与要求

You are preparing for the national entrance examination for MS/MA and are in need of some contact with Professor Li, your would-be tutor. Write a letter to him to

1）make a brief self-introduction,

2）state the reasons for the choice of your major and

3）outline your plan after graduation.

You should write about 100 words on ANSWER SHEET 2. Do not sign your own name at the end of the letter. Use "Li Ming" instead. You do not need to write the address. （10 points）

具体写作思路

1. 以一名要考研的大四学生的身份介绍自己。
2. 从来自西部农村的角度阐明报考计算机在农业领域应用这一专业的理由。
3. 从立志为家乡发展作贡献的角度解释毕业后的计划。

参考范文

A Letter of Self-introduction

Jan. 15, 2011

Dear Prof. Li,

I am a senior in the Computer Science Department of Tsinghua University. I am preparing for the national entrance exam and intend to pursue MS degree under your guidance, so I write to you for further information.

The reason for my application for the major—application of computer in farming— is quite simple. I am from the West. I was born and brought up in the countryside so that I intend to learn what can benefit the countryside.

After graduation, I want to make use of what I learn in university to make contribution to the development of my home-village, which is still one of the ten villages in poverty in our province.

I am looking forward to hearing from you.

Sincerely yours,

Li Ming

（130 words）

一句话点评

本文能够结合我国西部发展来展开写作难能可贵，使读者感受到强烈的情感冲击波。

全文翻译

一封自我介绍信

亲爱的李教授：

我是清华大学计算机科学系一名大四的学生。我正准备参加全国入学考试并且想要报考您的工学硕士研究生，因此给您写信询问更多的信息。

我选择计算机在农业方面应用这一专业的理由是非常简单的。我来自于西部。我出生并且成长在农村，因此我想要学习能够有益于农村的知识。

毕业后，我想利用自己在大学所学的知识为我的家乡发展作贡献，我的家乡目前还是我们省的十大贫困村之一。

我期待着您的回信。

真诚的

李明

2011 年 1 月 15 日

重点写作词语点睛

self-introduction 自我介绍	senior *n.* 大四的学生
pursue *v.* 寻求	application *n.* 应用
contribution *n.* 贡献	poverty *n.* 贫穷

考研英语应用文写作备考试题　　第 5 篇

写作题目与要求

Shao Bing, one of your colleagues, is planning to study English under Prof. Smith's guidance. Write a letter to Prof. Smith to

1）introduce Shao Bing,

2）clarify Shao Bing's plan, and

3）express your appreciation.

You should write about 100 words on ANSWER SHEET 2. Do not sign your own name at the end of the letter. Use "Li Ming" instead. You do not need to write the address. (10 points)

具体写作思路

1. 说明邵兵是自己的同事，他从复旦大学毕业，主修英语，毕业后一直教英语，工作出色。

2. 说明邵兵想要师从史密斯教授进修英语。

3. 对史密斯教授表示感谢。

参考范文

A Letter of Introduction

Jan. 15, 2011

Dear Prof. Smith,

I take pleasure in introducing Mr. Shao Bing to you, who is a colleague of mine in the English Department of Peking University. Mr. Shao Bing graduated from the English Department of Fudan University in 2006, majoring in English. Since then he has been teaching

English. Mr. Shao is a capable person who has made some outstanding achievements in his studies and work.

Mr. Shao now intends to prepare himself for further study of English. He would like to do some research under your direction.

I would greatly appreciate it if you would give Mr. Shao assistance and guidance.

With my personal regards,

Sincerely yours,

Li Ming

（111 words）

一句话点评

作者在第一段阐明自己与邵兵（被介绍人）之间的关系并且对邵兵进行全面而具体的介绍，这是介绍类信函所必需的写作手法。

全文翻译

一封介绍信

亲爱的史密斯教授：

我十分荣幸地向您介绍邵兵先生，他是我在北京大学英语系的一名同事。邵兵先生 2006 年毕业于复旦大学英语系，主修英语。毕业后他一直教英语。他是一位能人，在工作和研究中取得了显著的成绩。

邵兵先生打算进修英语。他想在您的指导下进行英语研究。

如果您能给邵兵先生帮助和指导，我将十分感激。

祝好！

真诚的

李明

2011 年 1 月 15 日

重点写作词语点睛

colleague	*n.* 同事	graduate from	从…毕业
major in	主修…专业	further study	进修
appreciate	*v.* 欣赏；感谢	guidance	*n.* 指导

考研英语应用文写作备考试题　　第 6 篇

写作题目与要求

You have taught Zhou Jie for two years. Write a letter of recommendation for Zhou Jie to

1) state your relationship with Zhou,

2) introduce Zhou's academic achievements,

3) introduce his language proficiency,

4) introduce his sports and social activities, and

5) express your sincere recommendation.

You should write about 100 words on ANSWER SHEET 2. Do not sign your own name at the end of the letter. Use "Li Ming" instead. You do not need to write the address. (10 points)

具体写作思路

1. 以老师的身份推荐周杰。

2. 说明周在数学和物理方面的出色表现。

3. 说明周的英语水平。

4. 说明周在体育等方面的能力。

5. 表示大力推荐周杰。

参考范文

A Letter of Recommendation

Jan. 15, 2011

To Whom it May Concern,

It is indeed a pleasure for me to write this letter of recommendation for Zhou Jie, a student of mine for the past two years in Peking University. During his four years study in our university, he has distinguished himself in this university, and shows great potential for future accomplishments.

Zhou is in the Math & Physics Enrichment Program of our university. His achievements in all his subjects place him among the top five percent of students in the grade.

Zhou is equally strong in language. His English proficiency has reached the level of CET 6.

Finally, Zhou is a model student. He is the captain of the school basketball team, and a member of several student organizations.

In conclusion, Zhou is one of the most gifted students I have had the pleasure to teach. He is most deserving of any opportunity you can give to him.

Very truly yours,

Li Ming

Dean of Computer Science Department

(164 words)

作者在第一段明确交代了与周杰的关系，这是推荐信所必须明确写出的内容。

全文翻译

一封推荐信

致有关人士：

我十分荣幸地为周杰写这封推荐信。周杰是我在北京大学近两年所教过的学生。在大学的四年中，周杰十分出色并且对未来取得成就显示出巨大的潜力。

周是我们大学数学和物理加强项目的成员。他在所有科目方面的成绩使他在全年级名列前茅。

他的语言能力也很强。他的英语水平达到 CET 六级。

还有，周是一名模范学生。他是校篮球队队长，还是若干学生组织的成员。

总之，周是我有幸教过的非常聪明的学生之一。他值得你们给予他任何机会。

真诚的

李明

计算机科学系主任

2011 年 1 月 15 日

重点写作词语点睛

distinguish *v.* 使杰出　　accomplishment *n.* 成就

subject *n.* 科目　　proficiency *n.* 精通

model *n.* 模范　　deserve *v.* 值得

考研英语应用文写作备考试题　　第 7 篇

写作题目与要求

You will graduate from university and intend to be a volunteer to go to the West of China. After reading a notice of recruitment, write a letter to president of your university to

1）express your wish to go to the West

2）state your reasons, and

3）depict your plan.

You should write about 100 words on ANSWER SHEET 2. Do not sign your own name at the end of the letter. Use "Li Ming" instead. You do not need to write the address. （10 points）

具体写作思路

1. 具体交代本人是针对 1 月 11 日一则招募西部志愿者启事而写的一封回信。
2. 以自己来自于西部并且西部仍然贫穷来阐述想要做志愿者的理由。
3. 说明自己的打算是在西部普及计算机知识。

参考范文

A Letter of Application

Jan. 15, 2011

Dear President,

I, the undersigned, am a senior in the Computer Science Department of our university. In response to the Notice of Recruitment on January 11, I write to you to express my sincere wish to be a volunteer to go the West.

The foremost reasons for my desire to be a volunteer can be briefed as follows. First of all, I am from the West so that I have a deep love for the West and the people there. What's more, the West is still underdeveloped and some people there still live in poverty.

I plan to put what I have learned in university into practice. To be exact, to popularize computer knowledge in the West is the uppermost in my thoughts.

I am looking forward to your reply.

Sincerely yours,

Li Ming

(137 words)

一句话点评

本文能够结合西部进行写作真实且感人，能够把祖国的命运和写作联系在一起是考研高分写作的关键。

全文翻译

一封申请信

亲爱的校长：

我是本校计算机科学系一名大四的学生。针对 1 月 11 日的招募启事，我给您写信表达我想做一名西部志愿者的希望。

我想做西部志愿者的主要原因简述如下。首先，我来自于西部，因此我对西部和那里的人们有着深深的爱。此外，西部仍然是一个不发达地区并且一些人仍然生活在贫困中。

我打算把我在大学所学的知识用于实践。准确地说，在西部普及计算机知识是我最想做的事情。

我期待着您的回复。

真诚的

李明

2011 年 1 月 15 日

重点写作词语点睛

recruitment	*n.* 征募	response	*n.* 回复
volunteer	*n.* 志愿者	poverty	*n.* 贫穷
popularize	*v.* 普及	the uppermost in my thoughts	首先思考的事情

考研英语应用文写作备考试题　　第 8 篇

写作题目与要求

You will graduate from university and are hunting for a job. After reading a job ad from *Talent Journal*, write a letter to the Personnel Department to

1) state your reason to write the application,

2) describe your relevant education background,

3) introduce your English level, and

4) state your way of contact.

You should write about 100 words on ANSWER SHEET 2. Do not sign your own name at the end of the letter. Use "Li Ming" instead. You do not need to write the address. (10 points)

具体写作思路

1. 以回复 2011 年 1 月 5 日《人才报》周日刊招聘生产协调员的广告展开第一段的写作。

2. 说明你将要大学毕业并获得学士学位，还接受过计算机培训。

3. 说明你通过了六级考试。

4. 表示你渴望面试的机会并且留下你的电话。

参考范文

A Letter of Application

Jan. 15, 2011

Dear Sir/Madam,

I am responding to your ad in the January 5th 2011, the Sunday issue of the *Talent*

Journal for the position of production coordinator. I feel that my background in electronics and manufacturing will fit in well.

I will graduate from the Beijing Science & Technology University in July with a Bachelor of Science degree in Manufacturing Engineering. I have had extensive training on computers while at school.

I passed CET-6 in 2007. Not only do I pay much attention to improving my reading and listening skills, but I also keep practicing oral English.

Would you please call me to set an interview? I can be reached at my resume address or by phoning (010) 8207-3660 after 4 p. m.

I am looking forward to hearing from you.

Sincerely yours,

Li Ming

（133 words）

一句话点评

本文中具体的招聘广告日期、所学专业、英语水平和电话号码是本文完美、真切的要素。

全文翻译

一封求职信

亲爱的女士/先生：

我是看到你们 2011 年 1 月 5 日在《人才报》周日刊所登的生产协调员招聘广告写这封应聘信的。我认为，我在电子学和制造学方面的教育背景可以胜任这个职位。

我将于七月从北京科技大学毕业，并获得制造工程专业的硕士学位。在校期间我还接受了广泛的计算机培训。

我在 2006 年通过了英语六级考试。我不仅注意提高我的阅读和听力能力，还不断练习口语。

你们会电话通知我面试时间吗？通过简历上的地址或在四点后拨打电话（010）82073660 就可以找到我。

我期待着你们的回复。

真诚的
李明
2011 年 1 月 15 日

重点写作词语点睛

application　*n.* 申请	respond　*v.* 回复
ad　*n.* 广告	issue　*n.* （报刊）期号
bachelor　*n.* 学士	interview　*n.* 面试

写作题目与要求

You will graduate from university and intend to continue your further study overseas. Write a letter to a graduate school to

1）make a self-introduction,

2）express your wish to get a place in the graduate school, and

3）ask for relevant documents.

You should write about 100 words on ANSWER SHEET 2. Do not sign your own name at the end of the letter. Use "Li Ming" instead. You do not need to write the address. （10 points）

具体写作思路

1. 以清华大学力学系主修流体力学大四学生的身份介绍自己。

2. 说明自己想要申请流体力学方面的硕士学位。

3. 索要有关专业资料、入学申请表和奖学金申请表。

参考范文

A Letter of Application

Jan. 15, 2011

Dear Sir/Madam,

I, the undersigned, am a senior in the Department of Mechanics at Tsinghua University. As an undergraduate, I major in fluid dynamics.

At present, I would like to apply for a place at your graduate school for studies in fluid dynamics leading to the degree of Master of Science.

By the way, could you send me some materials on my major and an application form for admission? I would also like to apply for scholarship. Could you please send me this application form as well?

Your assistance will be highly appreciated. I am looking forward to hearing from you.

Sincerely yours,

Li Ming

（105 words）

一句话点评

本文在第三段写作过程中所涉及的专业资料、入学申请表格和奖学金申请表具体翔实，使我们读起来逼真而具体。

一封申请信

亲爱的女士/先生：

我是清华大学力学系一名大四的学生。作为一名本科生，我主修流体力学。

目前，我想申请贵校研究生院流体力学方向的硕士研究生。

顺便说一句，您能寄给我有关专业方面的一些资料和入学申请表吗？我还想申请奖学金。您能寄给我奖学金申请表吗？

我将十分感谢您的帮助。我正期待着您的回复。

真诚的

李明

2011 年 1 月 15 日

重点写作词语点睛

undergraduate *n.* 本科生	major in 主修…专业
apply for 申请	admission *n.* 入学
scholarship *n.* 奖学金	assistance *n.* 帮助

考研英语应用文写作备考试题　第10篇

写作题目与要求

You are writing your graduation thesis and are in need of some reference materials. Write a letter to Prof. Smith in Harvard to

1）make a brief self-introduction,

2）state the reference materials you want, and

3）stress the importance of the material to you.

You should write about 100 words on ANSWER SHEET 2. Do not sign your own name at the end of the letter. Use "Li Ming" instead. You do not need to write the address. （10 points）

具体写作思路

1. 以一名大四学生的身份和正在写毕业论文为由进行自我介绍。

2. 说明自己索要的资料是有关计算机在北美学生中应用的内容，并且资料应涉及近 20 年的情况。

3. 点明索要的材料与论文写作的成与败之间的关系。

A Letter of Request

Jan. 15, 2011

Dear Prof. Smith,

I, the undersigned, am a senior in the Computer Science Department of Tsinghua University. At the moment, I am writing my graduation thesis and in urgent need of some reference materials so that I write to you for help.

The material on the application of computer among university students in North America is what I need most. Most importantly, the relevant statistics and reports should cover the past two decades. And all the materials must be publications of national level.

Moreover, I would like to highlight the importance of the material to me. The material which I ask you for will to some extent decide the failure or success of my graduation thesis since the title of my thesis is *Application of Computers on Campus Both at Home and Abroad over the Past Two Decades*. I have failed to find relevant up-to-date materials in China.

Your help would be much appreciated and I am looking forward to your reply.

Sincerely yours,

Li Ming

(166 words)

一句话点评

本文第二段中，有关索要资料的具体描述十分准确，使我们读起来非常清楚明白。

全文翻译

一封请求信

亲爱的史密斯教授：

我是清华大学计算机科学系一名大四的学生。现在，我正在写毕业论文，急需一些参考资料，故写信向您求助。

有关计算机在北美大学生中应用的资料是我非常需要的。重要的是，有关统计数字和报告应该覆盖近 20 年的情况。所有资料必须是国家级出版物。

此外，我想强调这些资料对我的重要性。我索取的资料将在某种程度上决定我论文的成败，因为我论文的题目是《近 20 年计算机在国内外校园的应用》。我在中国没有找到相关最新资料。

我将十分感谢您的帮助并期待您的回复。

真诚的

李明

2011 年 1 月 15 日

重点写作词语点睛

thesis   *n.* 论文

application   *n.* 应用

highlight   *v.* 强调

urgent   *a.* 急迫的

publication   *n.* 出版物

appreciate   *v.* 感谢

考研英语应用文写作备考试题　　第 11 篇

写作题目与要求

You are preparing for an English test and are in need of some reference books. Write a letter to the sales department of a bookstore to ask for：

1）detailed information about the books you want,

2）methods of payment,

3）time and way of delivery.

You should write about 100 words on ANSWER SHEET 2. Do not sign your own name at the end of the letter. Use "Li Ming" instead. You do not need to write the address.（10 points）

具体写作思路

1. 以一名大四的学生需要一本考研英语参考书为背景进行写作。

2. 具体询问《考研英语应用文写作》（*Practical Writing for NETEM*）一书的相关情况。

3. 是否可以通过网络付款。

4. 询问是否可以通过特快专递把书寄来。

参考范文

A Letter of Inquiry

Jan. 11, 2011

Dear Sales Manager,

I, the undersigned, am a senior in the Computer Science Department of Tsinghua University. At the moment, I am preparing for NETEM and need a reference book so that I write to you for help.

First of all, I am most interested in whether the book *Practical Writing for NETEM* is available in your Xinhua bookstore or not. By the way, do you offer any discount if I buy your book? Do you offer any free CD, VCD, DVD or MP3 concerning the book? Do you offer any free net-card?

Moreover, I would like to be informed about whether I can pay you for the book via network since my university is far away from your bookstore.

Last but not least important, I am also interested in whether you can deliver the book to me by way of EMS since I am in urgent need of the book, which will influence my score of NETEM.

I am looking forward to your early reply.

Sincerely yours,

Li Ming

（170 words）

一句话点评

本文围绕购买一本考研英语书进行应用文写作使本篇文章真实生动，这样的写作方法极易得高分。

全文翻译

一封问询信

亲爱的销售经理：

我是清华大学计算机科学系一名大四的学生。现在我正准备考研英语并需要一本参考书，故给您写信求助。

首先，我想知道你们书店是否出售《考研英语应用文写作》这本书。顺便问一句，你们是否打折？你们是否提供有关此书的 CD、VCD、DVD 或者 MP3？你们是否提供免费的网卡？

此外，我想知道是否可以通过网络付款，因为我们学校离书店很远。

最后但并非最不重要的一点，我想知道是否你们可以通过特快专递把书寄给我？我急需这本书，它将决定我的考研英语成绩。

我期待着您的回复。

真诚的

李明

2011 年 1 月 15 日

重点写作词语点睛

inquiry　*n.* 询问	reference　*n.* 参考
practical　*a.* 实用的	discount　*n.* 折扣
via　*prep.* 通过	EMS　特快专递服务

写作题目与要求

You and your family plan to make a two week trip to Tennessee, USA. Write a letter to the manager of a travel agency to

1）state your intention, ask for a brochure and a high-way map, and

2）express your appreciation.

You should write about 100 words on ANSWER SHEET 2. Do not sign your own name at the end of the letter. Use "Li Ming" instead. You do not need to write the address. (10 points)

具体写作思路

1. 告知有关 2010 年夏天到美国田纳西州进行两周旅行的计划，并请求对方寄来相关小册子和地图。

2. 针对对方的帮助表示感谢。

参考范文

A Letter of Request

Jan. 15, 2011

Dear Manager,

My family is planning a two-week trip through Tennessee during the summer of 2011. Please send a brochure or a pamphlet listing the scenic attractions of Eastern Tennessee and a highway map for the state. Because we are photography fans and avid hikers, we are interested specifically in geographic scenery, not man-made attractions.

Please send the two items to me at the address above. I understand this is a service you provide for those who plan vacations in the area, and I appreciate it.

We're looking forward to visiting your area in the United States.

Sincerely yours,

Li Ming

（105 words）

一句话点评

在第一段本文作者对所要索取的物品交代得十分细致具体，这种写作方法是请求类信函所不可缺少的手段。

一封请求信

亲爱的经理：

  我们的家庭正在计划 2011 年夏天到田纳西州进行为期两周的旅行。请劳驾寄给我有关田纳西州东部风景点的小册子和田纳西州的高速公路地图。因为我们是摄影和徒步旅行爱好者，所以我们对自然风景特别感兴趣，对人造的风景没有兴趣。

  请按上面地址给我寄来我要的两样资料。我知道这是你能为计划在该地区度假的人所提供的一种服务，特此感谢。

  我们期待着到美国你们的这个地区进行访问。

真诚的

李明

2011 年 1 月 15 日

重点写作词语点睛

request *n.* 请求	brochure *n.* 小册子
pamphlet *n.* 小册子	avid *a.* 劲头十足的
item *n.* 项目；物品	appreciate *v.* 感谢；欣赏

考研英语应用文写作备考试题　　第 13 篇

写作题目与要求

  You have received a letter of inquiry on application procedures of your university from Mr. Smith. Write a letter to him to

  1）tell him that you have received his letter,

  2）clarify the necessary steps in terms of guidelines for international applicants.

  You should write about 100 words on ANSWER SHEET 2. Do not sign your own name at the end of the letter. Use "Li Ming" instead. You do not need to write the address. （10 points）

具体写作思路

  1. 告知史密斯先生已经收到寄来的信。

  2. 具体指明申请北京科技大学所应注意的六点事项。

参考范文

A Letter of Advice

Jan. 15, 2011

Dear Mr. Smith,

Thank you for your <u>inquiry</u> on application <u>procedures</u> of Beijing University of Science and Technology. Here are some <u>guidelines</u> for international applicants:

(1) <u>Complete</u> the application form and make sure you have answered all the questions,

(2) Enclose your <u>HSK</u> score,

(3) Complete your personal essay,

(4) Enclose two letters of recommendation,

(5) Attach the following documents:

—Official <u>transcripts</u> from all the <u>institutions</u> you have attended,

—Financial statement, and

(6) Enclose a check of $150 application fee.

If you have any further questions, please do not hesitate to contact me.

Sincerely yours,

Li Ming

Admission Officer

(101 words)

一句话点评

在本文中作者所给出的指导十分详细而具体，这是建议指导类信函所必需的写作方式。

全文翻译

一封建议信

亲爱的史密斯先生：

感谢您来信询问有关北京科技大学申请入学手续方面的问题。下面是外国申请人所需要的步骤：

(1) 填写申请表并且确保回答所有问题；

(2) 随信寄来汉语水平考试成绩；

(3) 完成个人陈述；

(4) 随信寄来两封推荐信；

(5) 寄来下列资料：

——你所学习过的所有学校开出的学生成绩报告单，以及

——资金证明。

（6）随信寄来 150 美金的申请费用支票。

如果你还有问题，请一定与我联系。

真诚的

李明

录取官员

2011 年 1 月 15 日

重点写作词语点睛

inquiry　*n.* 询问	procedure　*n.* 手续
guideline　*n.* 指导	complete　*v.* 填写
HSK　汉语水平考试	transcript　*n.* 学生成绩报告单
institution　*n.* 机构	

考研英语应用文写作备考试题　　第 14 篇

写作题目与要求

Ms. Lewis has written a letter of inquiry to you, asking for ten-day group tour recommendation in the Shanghai region. Write a letter to her to

1）suggest your recommendation concerning Shanghai, Suzhou, Wuxi, and Hangzhou, and

2）clarify the relevant lodging and guide service.

You should write about 100 words on ANSWER SHEET 2. Do not sign your own name at the end of the letter. Use "Li Ming" instead. You do not need to write the address. （10 points）

具体写作思路

1. 具体讲出在上海、苏州、无锡和杭州所逗留的时间和建议参观的景点。
2. 说明住四星级酒店并且由有经验的导游陪同。

参考范文

A Letter of Recommendation

Jan. 15, 2011

Dear Ms. Lewis,

Thank you for contacting us for group tour recommendation in Shanghai region. Here is what our travel experts have come up with for a ten-day trip.

(1) Use Shanghai as your travel headquarters to other locations.

(2) Plan to spend four to five days in Shanghai. Scenery spots may include: the Shanghai Museum, the Tower of the Oriental Pearl, the Bund, and so forth.

(3) Plan a two-day trip to Suzhou and Wuxi, which are a one-hour ride away from Shanghai; Suzhou's gardens and Wuxi's Taihu Lake are the spots you can't miss.

(4) Plan another two-day trip to the scenic city of Hangzhou, which is a two-hour train ride away from Shanghai. Hangzhou's West Lake is a must-see place.

Finally, in all three cities the group will be staying in four-star hotels and be led by an experienced tour-guide. I hope you would like the itinerary we have proposed to you and please do not hesitate to contact me if you have any further questions.

Very truly yours,

Li Ming

Travel Advisor

(180 words)

一句话点评

本文所给出的推荐旅游城市和景点十分具体，这是推荐类信函所必不可少的写作方式。

全文翻译

一封建议信

亲爱的路易斯女士：

感谢你与我们联系询问有关在上海地区团队旅游的建议。这是我们旅游专家所给出的一个为期十天的旅游计划。

(1) 把上海作为到其他地点旅游的中心点。

(2) 计划在上海逗留四至五天。主要景点包括：上海博物馆、东方明珠、上海外滩等。

(3) 计划在苏州和无锡逗留两天，从上海到那里坐车需要一小时。苏州园林和无锡太湖是我们不能错过的景点。

(4) 计划在杭州住两天，从上海坐火车到杭州需要两个小时。杭州的西湖是一定要去的地方。

在所有三个城市将下榻四星级酒店并且由经验丰富的导游陪同。我希望你喜欢我们为你建议的旅游路线。如有问题，请和我联系。

真诚的

李明

旅游顾问

2011 年 1 月 15 日

recommendation　*n.* 推荐，介绍　　headquarters　*n.* 总部

the Bund　上海外滩　　tour guide　导游

itinerary　*n.* 旅行计划，预定行程　　propose　*v.* 建议

考研英语应用文写作备考试题　　第 15 篇

写作题目与要求

You will graduate from university in the summer of 2011 and have experienced ups and downs over the past four years. Write a letter to the freshmen to

1）state how to adapt oneself to campus life, and

2）stress the importance of English learning.

You should write about 100 words on ANSWER SHEET 2. Do not sign your own name at the end of the letter. Use "Li Ming" instead. You do not need to write the address. （10 points）

具体写作思路

1. 以西北大学一名大四学生的身份开启全篇。

2. 强调思想的改变是适应校园生活的关键，并且把中学和大学进行对比。

3. 围绕四级考试阐述英语学习的重要性。

参考范文

A Letter of Advice

Jan. 15, 2011

Dear Freshmen,

I, the undersigned, am a senior in the Computer Science Department of Northwest University. I would like to say a few words to you, which I hope would be helpful to you.

To begin with, the change of ideas is of most importance for freshmen to adapt themselves to campus life. During the middle school days, we usually depend upon our teachers at school and parents at home. However, the life and study on campus feature independence, which is essential to our psychological development. In my view, we had better always bear in mind the idea of independence.

What's more, English learning is a must. On one hand, without CET 4 certificate, we can not get our degree when we graduate. On the other hand, when we hunt for job, English level is a deciding factor. Therefore, I do hope that all of you will have a good understanding of the necessity of learning English well.

Good Luck to you!

Sincerely yours,

Li Ming

（166 words）

一句话点评

本文在叙述时的两个得分亮点是：学会独立和通过四级考试。

全文翻译

<h2 align="center">一封建议信</h2>

亲爱的大一新生：

我是西北大学计算机科学系大四的学生。我想对你们说几句话，我希望对你们有益。

首先，思想的改变对自己适应校园生活是非常重要的。在中学时，我们通常在学校依赖老师在家里依赖家长。然而，大学校园的生活和学习的特点是独立，这对心理发展是重要的。我认为，我们最好永远保持独立的意识。

此外，英语学习是必需的。一方面，没有四级证书，我们在毕业时就拿不到学位。另一方面，我们找工作时，英语是一个决定性因素。因此，我希望你们懂得英语学习的重要性。

祝你们好运！

真诚的

李明

2011 年 1 月 15 日

重点写作词语点睛

feature *v.* 以…为特色	psychological *a.* 心理的
independence *n.* 独立	certificate *n.* 证书
degree *n.* 学位	deciding *a.* 决定的

考研英语应用文写作备考试题　　第16篇

写作题目与要求

You have been ill and hospitalized for two weeks. Your teachers and classmates went to see you. Write a letter to them to

1）thank them for their coming to see you,

2）describe your feeling, and

3）state your present condition.

You should write about 100 words on ANSWER SHEET 2. Do not sign your own name at the end of the letter. Use "Li Ming" instead. You do not need to write the address. (10 points)

具体写作思路

1. 对老师和同学们在期末考试的紧张阶段抽出时间来探望自己表示感谢。
2. 阐述大家的探望给自己带来了战胜疾病的勇气并且赶走了孤独。
3. 谈论身体有较大的恢复并且不久就可以出院了。

参考范文

A Letter of Thanks

Jan. 15, 2011

Dear Teachers and Classmates,

First of all, please allow me to say "Thank you" to all of you. It is very kind of you to spare your valuable time during the period of final examinations and come to see me.

Your visit has given me much confidence and power to overcome the illness. When I first came to the hospital, I really felt lonely and did not have enough courage and confidence to overcome the illness. Your visit has made me feel that I am not poor and lonely in the world and in fact I am living in a world of love.

These days, my condition has been obviously improved due to the careful treatment offered by doctors and nurses. My doctor has told me that I will completely recover from illness in two weeks. I hope that I can see you earlier.

Again, special thanks go to all of you.

Sincerely yours

Li Ming

(166 words)

一句话点评

本文能够围绕自信心和孤独感进行分析和阐述，这使本文的写作内容变得比较深刻。

全文翻译

一封感谢信

亲爱的老师和同学们：

首先，请允许我向大家说一声"谢谢"。你们在期末考试阶段抽出时间来看望我真是太好了。

你们的探望给我带来了战胜疾病的信心和力量。我刚来到医院时，我真的感到孤独并且没有足够的勇气和信心去战胜疾病。你们的探望使我感觉到我在世界上不是可怜和孤独的，实际上我生活在爱的世界里。

近来，由于医生和护士精心的治疗，我的病情明显好转。医生告诉我两周之后我就完全康复了。我希望早日见到你们。

再一次衷心地感谢你们。

真诚的

李明

2011 年 1 月 15 日

重点写作词语点睛

spare	*v.* 抽出	overcome	*v.* 克服
lonely	*a.* 孤独的	courage	*n.* 勇气
treatment	*n.* 治疗	recover	*v.* 恢复

考研英语应用文写作备考试题　　第 17 篇

写作题目与要求

Prof. Smith has sent you the list of reference books which you asked for. Write a letter to him to

1）express your gratitude, and

2）depict your benefit from the list.

You should write about 100 words on ANSWER SHEET 2. Do not sign your own name at the end of the letter. Use "Li Ming" instead. You do not need to write the address. (10 points)

具体写作思路

1. 对老师给自己寄来参考书目单表示高兴和感谢。
2. 具体说明老师的帮助给自己节省了很多时间。
3. 再次对老师表示深深的感谢。

参考范文

A Letter of Thanks

Jan. 15, 2011

Dear Prof. Smith,

I am writing to tell you how very kind of you to send me the <u>list</u> of reference books.

They are exactly what I need for my thesis.

When I was going through the book list yesterday, I realized how much time you have saved for me. As a matter of fact, I have been looking for those books in the library for quite a while, but without too much luck. Now here they are in the mail from a mentor as well as a friend.

I feel deeply indebted to you and I really don't know how to thank you enough for your help.

Sincerely yours,

Li Ming

(114 words)

一句话点评

在第二段中所给出的感谢理由真实可信，这是应用文写作得高分的关键。

全文翻译

一封感谢信

亲爱的史密斯教授：

我写信以感谢您好心给我寄来了参考书目单。这正是我写论文所需要的。

昨天在阅读书单时，我意识到您帮我节省了大量的时间。实际上，我在图书馆一直寻找那些书，但没有找到。现在我的良师益友给我寄了过来。

我对您深表感激，不知如何感谢您的帮助。

真诚的

李明

2011 年 1 月 15 日

重点写作词语点睛

list *n.* 单子	thesis *n.* 论文
go through 仔细查看	as a matter of fact 实际上
mentor *n.* 良师益友	indebted *a.* 感激的

考研英语应用文写作备考试题　　第 18 篇

写作题目与要求

You and your sister spent your weekend at Mr. and Mrs. Johnson's country house. Write a letter to them to

153

1）express your gratitude, and

2）depict the importance of the weekend in terms of physical relaxation.

You should write about 100 words on ANSWER SHEET 2. Do not sign your own name at the end of the letter. Use "Li Ming" instead. You do not need to write the address. (10 points)

具体写作思路

1. 首先表明自己难忘在 New Hampshire Rocky Town 所度过的周末，并陈述原因。
2. 说明自己在那里得到了放松。
3. 表示感谢。

参考范文

A Letter of Thanks

Jan. 15, 2011

Dear Mr. and Mrs. Johnson,

I'd like you to know how much the weekend at your country house in Rocky Town, New Hampshire has meant to us. What you offered in the country is exactly what we have missed in the city — fresh air, green grass, blue sky, and singing birds. Most of all, however, is your kindness and hospitality.

We not only had a wonderful time, but also felt relaxed and refreshed completely. It has been a long time since we last enjoyed ourselves so thoroughly!

Many thanks to you for inviting both my sister and me.

Sincerely,

Li Ming

（105 words）

一句话点评

在第一段解释难忘的周末时，作者提到新鲜的空气、蓝天和鸣叫的鸟以及主人的热情好客，这一切都显得非常贴近我们的现实生活。感谢信的最大特点就是真诚和真实。

全文翻译

一封感谢信

亲爱的琼斯先生和琼斯夫人：

我想让你们知道在 New Hampshire Rocky Town 你们乡村的家里度过的周末对我们意味深长。在乡村你们所提供的一切正是我们在城市所没有的——新鲜的空气、蓝天和鸣叫的鸟。

然而，最重要的是你们的热情好客。

我们不仅度过了美好的时光，更感到彻底的放松和振奋。我们很久没有这样彻底地放松了！

多谢你们邀请我和我妹妹。

真诚的

李明

2011 年 1 月 15 日

重点写作词语点睛

offer	*v.* 提供	country	*n.* 乡村
hospitality	*n.* 热情好客	relaxed	*a.* 放松的
refreshed	*a.* 恢复精力的	thoroughly	*ad.* 彻底地

考研英语应用文写作备考试题　　第 19 篇

写作题目与要求

You have made an appointment with Prof. Wang, but failed to keep it. Write a letter to your teacher to

1）apologize for your failure to keep the appointment,

2）explain your reason to your teacher, and

3）express your wish to make another appointment.

You should write about 100 words on ANSWER SHEET 2. Do not sign your own name at the end of the letter. Use "Li Ming" instead. You do not need to write the address. (10 points)

具体写作思路

1. 深刻地为自己失约而表示道歉。

2. 讲述自己失约的理由是因为帮助一位因心脏病发作而晕倒的妇女。

3. 表达希望再次约会的愿望。

参考范文

A Letter of Apology

Jan. 15, 2011

Dear Prof. Wang,

First of all, please allow me to express my deep sorry for not being able to keep our appointment. I do know that this is very impolite and must have caused you much trouble.

I do reckon that at present any explanation is pale and futile. However I do not want you

155

to misunderstand me. On my way to your office, an old lady suddenly <u>fainted</u> due to <u>heart</u> <u>attack</u> on the bus. I stopped a taxi and sent her into a nearby hospital. I stayed there until her son came, which spoiled our appointment.

I am aware that our appointment is of importance. I do hope that you would be kind enough to spare your valuable time to meet me.

I am looking forward to hearing from you.

Sincerely yours,

Li Ming

(132 words)

一句话点评

把救助一位老妇人的事情当作违约的理由既真实感人又有说服力。

全文翻译

一封道歉信

亲爱的王教授：

首先，请允许我因为未能赴约而表示深深歉意。我知道这是十分无礼的，并且给您造成了很大的不便。

我的确认为现在任何解释都是苍白和无用的。然而，我不想让您误解我。在去您办公室的路上，一位老妇人因心脏病发作而晕倒在公共汽车上。我拦了一辆出租车并把老人送到附近的医院。我在医院一直等到老人的儿子到来。这打乱了我们的约会。

我知道我们的约会是重要的。我真的希望您能足以宽容并抽出宝贵时间面见我。

我期待着您的回复。

真诚的

李明

2011 年 1 月 15 日

重点写作词语点睛

apology　*n.* 道歉	appointment　*n.* 约会
reckon　*v.* 认为	futile　*a.* 无用的
faint　*a.* 晕倒	heart attack　心脏病

考研英语应用文写作备考试题　　第 20 篇

写作题目与要求

You can not keep the appointment you and Mr. Smith have made due to your English class. Write a letter to him to

    1）inform him of your case, and

    2）offer two other dates for your appointment.

You should write about 100 words on ANSWER SHEET 2. Do not sign your own name at the end of the letter. Use "Li Ming" instead. You do not need to write the address.（10 points）

具体写作思路

    1. 具体说明由于英语课的时间改变你不能于 2 月 22 日晚 7:30 赴约，并说明理由。

    2. 建议 2 月 25 日或 2 月 28 日见面。

参考范文

A Letter of Apology

Jan. 15, 2011

Dear Mr. Smith,

    I am very sorry to say that I will be unable to meet you on Wednesday, February 22 at 7:30 p.m. Unfortunately, I have English class at that time. The date of the class is changed because of the New Year's holidays.

    If it is possible I would like to see you some other time. I am free on Saturday evening February 25, or on Tuesday evening February 28. I hope one of these dates is convenient for you. Just let me know what is a better time for you. Please call me in the evenings.

    I am looking forward to seeing you.

Sincerely yours,

Li Ming

（115 words）

一句话点评

    在第一段对于自己不能赴约的原因解释的非常具体，这是道歉信所需要的写作手段。

全文翻译

一封道歉信

亲爱的史密斯先生：

    我非常抱歉地说我无法在 2 月 22 日（星期三）晚 7:30 与您见面。不走运的是，我有英语课。英语课的日期由于新年假日被改动。

如果可能的话我愿意改日见您。我在 2 月 25 日（星期六）晚或 2 月 28 日（星期二）晚有时间。希望这两个日期当中的一个对您合适。请让我知道哪一个时间更适合于您。请在晚上给我打电话。

期待着见到您。

真诚的

李明

2011 年 1 月 15 日

重点写作词语点睛

apology	*n.* 道歉	unfortunately	*ad.* 不幸地
date	*n.* 日期	holiday	*n.* 假日
convenient	*a.* 方便的	look forward to	期待

考研英语应用文写作备考试题　　第 21 篇

写作题目与要求

You did not attend Prof. Smith's class and failed to hand in your paper due to your illness. Write a letter to him to

1) apologize for your action,

2) ask for extension, and

3) promise to make up the lessons.

You should write about 100 words on ANSWER SHEET 2. Do not sign your own name at the end of the letter. Use "Li Ming" instead. You do not need to write the address. (10 points)

具体写作思路

1. 明确表示因缺课和未按时交作业而道歉，并且说明自己的理由是生病。
2. 请求老师延长交论文的时间并保证下周一定交上。
3. 告诉老师自己正在借助别人的课堂笔记来补课。

参考范文

A Letter of Apology

Jan. 15, 2011

Dear Prof. Smith,

I am writing to <u>apologize</u> for missing your class yesterday and for not <u>handing in</u> the paper <u>due</u> yesterday. I have been sick since last week, having a fever and a very bad cough.

158

Apparently, I am another victim of the recent flu.

Could you kindly <u>extend</u> the due date for my <u>paper</u> to next week? I have been working on it and I promise by next week the paper will be in your mailbox.

I will <u>catch up with</u> the lecture I missed today with the help of my roommate. He has left all the notes for me already.

Sincerely yours,

Li Ming

(110 words)

一句话点评

在第一段中所给出的道歉理由真实可信，这是道歉信所不可缺少的内容。

全文翻译

一封道歉信

亲爱的史密斯教授：

我给您写信表达我因昨天缺课和未按时交昨天到期的作业而感到的歉意。自从上周我一直生病，发烧、咳嗽得很严重。很明显我是最近流感的受害者。

您能延长我交论文的时间到下一周吗？我一直在完成论文并且保证下周将论文放到您的邮箱。

我将借助于室友的笔记补上我落下的课。室友已经把笔记留给我。

真诚的

李明

2011 年 1 月 15 日

重点写作词语点睛

apologize *v.* 道歉	hand in 交
due *a.* 到期的	extend *v.* 延长
paper *n.* 论文	catch up with … 赶上

考研英语应用文写作备考试题　　第 22 篇

写作题目与要求

You have been absent from Prof. Smith's class for two weeks. Write a letter to him to

1) state your reasons for absence, and

2) promise to make up the lessons.

You should write about 100 words on ANSWER SHEET 2. Do not sign your own name at the end of the letter. Use "Li Ming" instead. You do not need to write the address. (10 points)

具体写作思路

1. 因连续两周未上课进行解释，原因是回家看望生病的母亲。
2. 向老师表示将尽力把耽误的课补上。

参考范文

A Letter of <u>Explanation</u>

Jan. 15, 2011

Dear Prof. Smith,

Please allow me to explain why I have been absent from your lectures two weeks in a <u>row</u>. On Sunday two weeks ago, I received a call from my sister saying that my mother was very sick in the hospital and had to receive an operation. Since my mother is very dear to me, I had to <u>rush back</u> to our home in Inner Mongolia and be at her sick bedside.

<u>Now that</u> I am back on campus, I am <u>making up</u> all the lessons I missed during the two-week absence from school. I can assure you that I am catching up with all the reading and <u>assignments</u>.

With regards.

Very sincerely,
Li Ming
（120 words）

一句话点评

在第一段所给出的解释理由真实动人，这是解释信函所不可缺少的内容。

全文翻译

一封解释信

亲爱的史密斯先生：

请允许我向您解释我连续两周没有上课的原因。两周前的星期六，我接到我姐姐的电话说我妈妈生病住院不得不做手术。因为我很爱妈妈，我必须赶回内蒙古的家并守候在母亲的病床旁。

现在，我回到学校。我正在补这两周耽误的课业。我保证完成阅读材料和作业。

祝好！

真诚的
李明
2011 年 1 月 15 日

explanation   *n.* 解释   row   *n.* 连续
rush back   迅速返回   now that   既然
make up   弥补   assignment   *n.* 作业

考研英语应用文写作备考试题   第 23 篇

写作题目与要求

You are preparing for an English test and have ordered a reference book from a bookstore. After you read the book, you found that it is a pirated one（盗版书）. Write a letter to the sales department of the bookstore to

1）state your case,

2）depict the negative effect, and

3）ask for compensation.

You should write about 100 words on ANSWER SHEET 2. Do not sign your own name at the end of the letter. Use "Li Ming" instead. You do not need to write the address. (10 points)

具体写作思路

1. 以一名大四的学生定购《考研英语应用文写作和阅读》（Practical Writing and Reading for NETEM）的事例陈述自己的情况。

2. 围绕该书字迹难以辨认和答案有误两点来阐述给自己带来的不良影响。

3. 明确提出退还书款的要求。

参考范文

A Letter of Complaint

Jan. 15, 2011

Dear Sales Manager,

I, the undersigned, am a senior in the Computer Science Department of Tsinghua University. I ordered a book which is entitled *Practical Writing and Reading for NETEM* by Wang Li on December 20th, 2010. However after reading the book on January 5th, 2011, I found that it is a pirated one so that I write to you for complaint.

The book has brought me some negative effects. To begin with, much of my valuable time and energy have been wasted in reading the book since it is quite hard to identify many words in the book. What's more, I have not benefited from reading the book since some of the keys to the exercises are <u>misprinted</u>.

I would like to be informed whether you can refund me the money.

I am looking forward to your early reply.

Sincerely yours,

Li Ming

（144 words）

一句话点评

本文所涉及的书名（即《考研英语应用文写作和阅读》）使本文显得真实具体，使我们在阅读本文时有一种亲切感。

全文翻译

一封投诉信

亲爱的销售经理：

我是清华大学计算机科学系一名大四的学生。我在 2010 年 12 月 20 日定购了一本王力编写的《考研英语应用文写作和阅读》。然而，我在 2011 年 1 月 5 日读完此书后发现这是一本盗版书，故写信投诉。

该书给我带来了一些不利影响。首先，在阅读此书时，浪费了我的大量宝贵时间和精力，因为本书的许多单词难以辨认。此外，因为练习的一些答案印错，我从阅读中没有受益。

我希望被告知是否您能退给我书款。

我期待着您的答复。

真诚的

李明

2011 年 1 月 15 日

重点写作词语点睛

complaint	*n.* 投诉	pirate	*v.* 非法翻印
negative	*a.* 消极的	identify	*v.* 识别
misprint	*v.* 印错		

考研英语应用文写作备考试题　　第 24 篇

写作题目与要求

You have bought a washing machine, but it does not work. Write a letter to the manager of the store to

1）state your case, and

2）suggest your solution to the problem.

You should write about 100 words on ANSWER SHEET 2. Do not sign your own name at the end of the letter. Use "Li Ming" instead. You do not need to write the address. （10 points）

具体写作思路

1. 确切表明买了一台洗衣机，该机有故障。

2. 提出自己想要退款。

参考范文

A Letter of Complaint

Jan. 15, 2011

Dear Manager,

Last week I bought a washing machine at your store and when I got it home it did not work. When I tried to return it to the store, I was told that I could not get my money back.

The sign in your store says that money is refunded within 7 days and I returned my goods within that time. I insist that you return the money and take back the damaged washing machine. If I do not get a satisfactory response soon, I will complain to the Consumer Protection Association.

Please contact me at （010）82073660.

Sincerely,

Li Ming

（106 words）

一句话点评

在第一段中作者对自己所购买物品以及该物品的问题交代得十分清晰，这种清晰的交代方法是投诉信第一段所必备的要素。

全文翻译

一封投诉信

尊敬的经理：

上周我在你们商店买了一台洗衣机。当我把洗衣机运到家时，发现它无法运转。当我到商店试图退货时，商店告诉我说无法退款。

你们商店的牌子上写着七天内可以退款，我是在这个期限内退货的。我坚持让你们退款并拿回受损的洗衣机。如果我不能很快得到一个满意的答复，我将投诉到消费者保护协会。

我的电话是 010-82073660。

真诚的

李明

2011 年 1 月 15 日

重点写作词语点睛

sign *n.* 招牌；标志	refund *v.* 退款
insist *v.* 坚持	damage *v.* 损害
complain *v.* 投诉	association *n.* 协会

考研英语应用文写作备考试题　第 25 篇

写作题目与要求

You have received a letter of complaint for an electronic dictionary from Mr. Williams. Write a letter to him to

1) express your pity on hearing his complaint,

2) state three ways to solve his problem, and

3) ask him to make a choice on the enclosed postcard.

You should write about 100 words on ANSWER SHEET 2. Do not sign your own name at the end of the letter. Use "Li Ming" instead. You do not need to write the address. (10 points)

具体写作思路

1. 表示因收到对方有关电子辞典的投诉而感到不安。
2. 具体阐明解决的三种办法。
3. 请对方回复用何种方法解决此事。

参考范文

A Responding Letter to Complaint

Jan. 15, 2011

Dear Mr. Williams,

We are disturbed to learn that the electronic dictionary you recently bought from us did not work well. We want our customers to be satisfied and that is why we have a policy of guaranteed satisfaction.

There are three ways we can handle this situation: (1) we can replace the dictionary; (2) we can give you a full refund; or (3) you can apply the amount to any other merchandise in our store.

Please indicate your preference on the enclosed postcard and also write in the date when we can pick up the unsatisfactory dictionary. Pickups are made in the mornings.

We value your business and friendship.

Yours very truly,

Li Ming

Manager of Sales Department

(122 words)

一句话点评

在第二段中，本文具体交代了解决投诉的三种方法，这种详细交代解决投诉方法的写作手法是回复投诉信的一个重要环节。

全文翻译

一封有关投诉的回复信

尊敬的威廉姆斯先生：

得知您最近从我处购买的电子辞典不能正常使用，我们感到十分不安。我们想让顾客满意，这正是为什么我们拥有保证满意的政策。

有三种方法处理这件事情：一，我们可以调换辞典；二，我们可以给你全额退款；三，你可以用这笔钱来购买我们商店的其他商品。

请在随信所附的明信卡上注明你喜欢的解决方法，并告知我们取回有故障辞典的日期。登门取货一般在上午。

我们重视与您的商务往来和友谊。

真诚的

李明

销售部经理

2011 年 1 月 15 日

重点写作词语点睛

disturb   v. 使心神不安   guarantee   v. 保证
refund   n. 退款   merchandise   n. 商品
indicate   v. 指出   pick up   取

写作题目与要求

As a sales representative in charge of distribution of electronic alarm system, write a letter to Ms Lewis to

1) state the purpose of your letter,

2) introduce the advantage and function of your product,

3) express your willingness to make a demonstration, and

4) offer your way of contact.

You should write about 100 words on ANSWER SHEET 2. Do not sign your own name at the end of the letter. Use "Li Ming" instead. You do not need to write the address. (10 points)

具体写作思路

1. 具体说明自己是国美电器家用电子警报系统的销售代表。

2. 说明该系统易操作、难破坏等优点。

3. 说明十分钟就可以展示该系统的性能。

4. 留自己的联系电话。

参考范文

A Letter of Promotion

Jan. 15, 2011

Dear Ms Lewis,

I am a sales representative of Gome Electronic Warehouse. I am writing to find if you are interested in a new high-tech house electronic alarm system which our company has just distributed.

The system is easy to be controled by house holder and hard to be destroyed. The system protects your house round the clock.

If you would give me 10 minutes of your valuable time, I could demonstrate you the effectiveness of the new alarm system. You have no obligation to buy, but if you decide to order, the installation fee will be waived.

If you are interested, please call toll-free 1-800-8207-3660 and I will be more than happy to do a demo at your home.

Very sincerely yours,

Li Ming

(126 words)

本义在第一段和第二段分别详细介绍了产品名称和主要性能，这是推销类信函所必需的写作方式。

全文翻译

一封推销信

亲爱的路易斯女士：

我是国美电器的一名销售代表。我写信向您了解是否对我公司刚刚开始销售的高科技新型电子警报系统有兴趣。

这种系统容易操控，而且不易被破坏。该系统 24 小时保护您的家。

如果您给我十分钟的宝贵时间，我能够向您展示警报系统的功效。您不必一定购买，但是如果您决定订购，可以免除安装费。

如果您感兴趣，请拨免费咨询电话 1-800-8207-3660。我将十分高兴上门为您进行展示。

真诚的

李明

2011 年 1 月 15 日

重点写作词语点睛

representative *n.* 代表	Gome Electronic Warehouse 国美电器
alarm system 警报系统	round the clock 24 小时
obligation *n.* 义务	order *v.* 定购
waive *v.* 免除	toll-free 免费拨打的
demo *n.* 展示	

考研英语应用文写作备考试题   第 27 篇

写作题目与要求

The Spring Festival is coming shortly. You intend to invite Beckham, your foreign friend, to come to China and spend the traditional Chinese Festival together. Write a letter to him to

1）express your invitation to him,

2）introduce the Spring Festival, and

3）mention the places you will accompany him to visit.

You should write about 100 words on ANSWER SHEET 2. Do not sign your own name at the end of the letter. Use "Li Ming" instead. You do not need to write the address. (10 points)

具体写作思路

1. 明确表示邀请朋友在春节时来中国。
2. 说明中国人重视春节，春节是中国最重要的节日，并且把春节和圣诞节进行比较。
3. 具体指明陪朋友到集市去观赏中国传统文化。

参考范文

A Letter of Invitation

Jan. 15, 2011

Dear Beckham,

First of all, please allow me to express my heartfelt invitation to you. Since the Spring Festival is coming shortly, I sincerely invite you to come to China and spend the holiday with me.

The Spring Festival is of much importance to Chinese people. It has a long history and Chinese has been thinking highly of the holiday. To be exact, the Spring Festival has been the most significant holiday. What the Spring Festival means to Chinese is the same as Christmas means to the Westerners.

If you come, I am going to accompany you to fairgrounds, where you can have a close look at some of the Chinese traditional culture.

I am looking forward to your reply.

Sincerely yours,

Li Ming

(119 words)

一句话点评

把春节和圣诞节进行比较，这是一种恰当且行之有效的思想表达方式。

全文翻译

一封邀请信

亲爱的贝克汉姆：

首先，请允许我表达对你的诚挚邀请。因为春节马上就要到来，我诚挚地邀请你到中国来和我一起欢度春节。

春节对中国人而言是重要的。春节有着悠久的历史，中国人非常重视这个节日。准确地说，春节一直是最重要的节日。春节对中国人的意义就如同圣诞节和西方人的关系。

如果你来，我打算陪你到集市上去逛逛，在那里你可以看到一些中国传统文化。

我期待着你的回信。

真诚的

李明

2011 年 1 月 15 日

重点写作词语点睛

invitation	*n.* 邀请	heartfelt	*a.* 衷心的
think highly of	重视	fairground	*n.* 集市
traditional	*a.* 传统的	reply	*n.* 回复

考研英语应用文写作备考试题　　第 28 篇

写作题目与要求

On behalf of Student Union, you invite Prof. Smith to attend the anniversary of your university. Write a letter to him to

1）express your invitation,

2）state the reasons for your invitation, and

3）express your wish for his acceptance.

You should write about 100 words on ANSWER SHEET 2. Do not sign your own name at the end of the letter. Use "Li Ming" instead. You do not need to write the address.（10 points）

具体写作思路

1. 具体说明邀请史密斯教授于 3 月 7 日（星期一）出席由学生会主办的南方大学周年庆典招待会。

2. 说明邀请史密斯教授的理由：他曾在该校讲授十年的英语和文学；关注该校的活动。

3. 请求史密斯教授接受为期一天的邀请。

参考范文

A Letter of Invitation

Jan. 15, 2011

Dear Prof. Smith,

On Monday, March 7th, we are planning to have a reception to celebrate the anniversary of China Southern University and I have been asked by the Student Union to invite you to be the guest of honor on this occasion.

We learn that you had taught English language and literature in our university for over 10 years. Besides, you have always shown great interest in our activities. Therefore you are without doubt the ideal speaker.

We shall all be delighted as well as honored if you can find time to spend one day with us. I will send further details as soon as I hear from you. I hope that you will accept this invitation.

Sincerely,

Li Ming

President

Student Union of China Southern University

（131 words）

一句话点评

在第一段中，作者对时间、地点和活动的介绍具体而准确，这是邀请信不可缺少的内容。

全文翻译

一封邀请信

亲爱的史密斯教授：

在 3 月 7 日（星期一），我们计划举行南方大学周年庆典招待会。学生会委托我邀请您届时担任嘉宾。

我们知道您在我们学校讲授了十年的英语和文学。此外，您一直关注我们的活动。因此，毫无疑问您是理想的发言人。

如果您能抽时间和我们共度一天的时光，我们将十分高兴和荣幸。我一收到您的回复就会发给您进一步详细的信息。我希望您接受这个邀请。

真诚的

李明

南方大学学生会主席

2011 年 1 月 15 日

重点写作词语点睛

invitation	*n.* 邀请	reception	*n.* 招待会
anniversary	*n.* 周年纪念日	Student Union	学生会
guest of honor	贵宾	occasion	*n.* 时机

写作题目与要求

You can not accept the invitation by Mr. Smith with Cambridge University due to illness. Write a letter to him to

1）express your appreciation for his invitation，state your reason for declination，and

2）express your pity.

You should write about 100 words on ANSWER SHEET 2. Do not sign your own name at the end of the letter. Use "Li Ming" instead. You do not need to write the address.（10 points）

具体写作思路

1. 具体指出本人是回复 12 月 25 日的来信，该信邀请本文作者 2 月 27 日在剑桥大学周年纪念上做讲演。表明自己由于两周前患急性肺炎住院而无法接受邀请。

2. 对拒绝邀请表示抱歉并且对周年纪念表示祝贺。

参考范文

A Letter of Declination

Jan. 15，2011

Dear Mr. Smith，

Thank you for your letter of December 25，inviting me to give a speech on February 27 at the anniversary of Cambridge University. Apparently you have not heard that about two weeks ago I suffered from acute pneumonia and had to stay in the hospital for a number of days. Although I feel much better now，the doctor has advised me to take complete rest for at least one month.

In view of this，I regret that I am unable to accept your kind invitation to give the speech. I would like，however，to send my best wishes and congratulations to you on your anniversary.

Sincerely，

Li Ming

（111 words）

一句话点评

作者在第一段中所给出的拒绝理由具体真切，这是拒绝邀请信中所不可缺少的要素。

全文翻译

一封拒绝信

亲爱的史密斯先生：

感谢您 12 月 25 日的来信，邀请我于 2 月 27 日剑桥大学周年纪念上发表讲演。显然你没听说我在两周前患急性肺炎并且不得不住院许多天。虽然我现在好多了，医生仍建议我彻底休息一个月。

鉴于上述原因，我抱歉无法接受您的讲演邀请。但是，我对周年纪念送上最真诚的祝愿和祝贺。

真诚的

李明

2011 年 1 月 15 日

重点写作词语点睛

declination *n.* 拒绝	anniversary *n.* 周年纪念日
acute *a.* 急性的	pneumonia *n.* 肺炎
in view of 由于	congratulation *n.* 祝贺

考研英语应用文写作备考试题　第 30 篇

写作题目与要求

Over the past years, we have witnessed destructions of various kinds caused by human actions. As a university student, write a letter to our society to

1）enumerate present severe condition,

2）state the necessity of social concern, and

3）suggest counter-measures.

You should write about 100 words on ANSWER SHEET 2. Do not sign your own name at the end of the letter. Use "Li Ming" instead. You do not need to write the address. （10 points）

具体写作思路

1. 利用洪水、干旱、泥石流、沙尘暴和海啸等灾难来列举人类所面临的自然灾难。

2. 从地球是人类的家园、是我们获得衣食住行必需品的来源等原因来阐述保护地球的重要性。

3. 从立法的角度提出应对措施。

A Letter of Appeal

Jan. 15, 2011

To everyone on our planet,

Over the past years, floods, droughts, landslides, and dust-storms have frequented our planet — the only habitat of human beings. In December, 2004, tsunami（海啸）swept the South Asia, which has caused enormous damage. All these have sounded an alarm to human beings.

The destruction which is caused by human beings should arouse people's concern all over the world. If we take no heed of the present destructive human activities, our planet will become a tomb instead of a cozy home. What's more, we should realize that only from our planet can we obtain our sheltering, food, clothing and other daily necessities.

Counter-measures must be taken to curb the destruction caused by human beings. Most importantly, laws must be established to punish those who are involved in destructive conducts.

Yours,

Li Ming

（136 words）

一句话点评

在写作中能够提到重大灾难海啸使本文增色不少，利用最新的事实和数据是高分写作的关键。

全文翻译

一封呼吁信

致我们星球上的每一个人：

近年来，洪水、干旱、泥石流和沙尘暴经常光顾我们的星球——人类唯一的栖息地。2004年12月海啸席卷南亚，造成巨大的灾难。所有这些都给人类敲响了警钟。

人类所造成的破坏应该唤起全世界人们的关注。如果我们不注意目前人类破坏性的活动，我们的星球将变成坟墓而不是舒适的家园。此外，我们应该认识到只有从我们的星球我们才能获得我们的衣食住和其他日常必需品。

应该采取应对措施来抑制人类所造成的破坏。重要的是，一定要立法惩罚那些从事破坏活动的人。

真诚的

李明

2011年1月15日

重点写作词语点睛

appeal　*n.* 呼吁	frequent　*v.* 时常出入于
habitat　*n.* 栖息地	arouse　*v.* 唤起
concern　*n.* 关注	tomb　*n.* 坟墓

考研英语应用文写作备考试题　第31篇

写作题目与要求

On the occasion of the Spring Festival, write a letter of appeal to

1) inform the public of AIDS children's predicament,

2) ask people to make financial donation, and

3) state the requirements concerning donation.

You should write about 100 words on ANSWER SHEET 2. Do not sign your own name at the end of the letter. Use "Li Ming" instead. You do not need to write the address. (10 points)

具体写作思路

1. 说明艾滋病儿童生活在噩梦里。

2. 明确呼吁同学为艾滋病儿童捐款。

3. 说明捐款人要填写此信下方的表格，并告知捐款日期最好在 2011 年 2 月 10 日之前。

参考范文

A Letter of Appeal

Jan. 15, 2011

Dear Schoolmates,

The Spring Festival is approaching but AIDS children are living a nightmare. They dread the holiday season, knowing it might be their last.

Right now, schoolmates, you can help to bring a few moments of joy to AIDS children by making a financial donation to the China AIDS Foundation.

Please fill out the bottom portion of this letter and return it to us soon. Anything you can send before February 10, 2011 will be a great help. I know you'll do whatever you can. On behalf of the children, thank you for your care.

Sincerely yours,

Li Ming

(103 words)

在第二段作者明确呼吁同学为艾滋病儿童捐款并指出捐款至中国艾滋病基金会。这是一种非常有针对性的、非常明确的写作手法。这种写作手法是呼吁类信函所不可缺少的要素。

全文翻译

一封呼吁信

亲爱的同学们：

春节将至，但艾滋病儿童却生活在噩梦之中。他们害怕节日，认为这也许是他们的最后一个春节。

现在，同学们你们能够通过向中国艾滋病基金会捐款来给艾滋病儿童带来片刻的快乐。

请填写此信下方部分并且给我们寄回。2011 年 2 月 10 日之前你能寄来的款项将是巨大的帮助。我知道你们将尽自己所能。我代表这些儿童对你们的关心表示感谢。

真诚的

李明

2011 年 1 月 15 日

重点写作词语点睛

approach	v. 接近	nightmare	n. 噩梦
dread	v. 害怕	donation	n. 捐款
foundation	n. 基金	fill out	填写
portion	n. 部分	on behalf of	代表…

考研英语应用文写作备考试题　　第 32 篇

写作题目与要求

As an undergraduate, you have found some problems in terms of teaching in your university. Write a letter to your president to

1）state the purpose of your letter,

2）clarify the problems you have found,

3）state the negative effects, and

4）call for relevant investigation.

You should write about 100 words on ANSWER SHEET 2. Do not sign your own name at the end of the letter. Use "Li Ming" instead. You do not need to write the address. (10 points)

具体写作思路

1. 介绍自己是本校教育学院一名本科生，并说明自己写信的目的是有关教学质量。
2. 明确指出全职教师太少，自己所选的四门课几乎全部是兼职教师或助教授课。
3. 分析兼职教师所带来的不良后果。
4. 强烈提出校方应该调查此事。

参考范文

A Letter of Appeal

Jan. 15, 2011

Dear President,

I am an <u>undergraduate</u> in the School of Education. I have several <u>concerns</u> about the quality of teaching in our university.

I have discovered recently that very few of our instructors are full-time professors; in fact this year all four courses that I am taking are taught by either part-time professors or assistants.

I am not saying that the part-time instructors are not good teachers, but they have their <u>limitations</u>. They have no offices. As a result, they can't <u>assign</u> office hours for students. They are not well informed of many school regulations and events since they only come during class hours. They have little time to hear our questions and give advice, for they have neither space nor time for us.

Considering the fact that we <u>pay big bucks</u> to attend this university, don't we <u>deserve</u> some good teaching? I am looking forward to your reply.

Sincerely,

Li Ming

（155 words）

一句话点评

作者在第一段中对写信的目的和在第四段中对不良后果的分析细致具体，这是呼吁或建议类信件普遍具有的写作风格和要素。

全文翻译

一封呼吁信

亲爱的校长：

我是本校教育学院的一名本科生。我有关于本校教学质量的若干问题向您汇报。

我最近发现教师中很少的人是全职教师，实际上今年我选的四门课或者是兼职教师上课或者是助教上课。

我不是说兼职教师不是好老师。而是说他们有局限性。他们没有办公室，其结果是他们不能为学生留出办公室交流时间。他们不十分清楚许多学校的制度和事情，因为他们只是上课时才到学校来。因为他们没有空间或时间，所以他们没有时间来倾听学生的问题并且给出建议。

我们付了很多钱来上大学，难道我们不应该有一些良好的教育吗？我期待着您的回复。

真诚的

李明

2011 年 1 月 15 日

重点写作词语点睛

undergraduate　*n.* 本科生	concern　*n.* 关心，关注
limitation　*n.* 局限性	assign　*v.* 留出
pay big bucks　花许多钱	deserve　*v.* 值得

考研英语应用文写作备考试题　　第 33 篇

写作题目与要求

Li Peng, your younger brother, has graduated from high school and is admitted to Computer Science Department of Tsinghua University. Write a letter to him to

1）express your congratulations on him,

2）assess his feat, and

3）send him an air-ticket as gift.

You should write about 100 words on ANSWER SHEET 2. Do not sign your own name at the end of the letter. Use "Li Ming" instead. You do not need to write the address. （10 points）

具体写作思路

1. 祝贺李朋高中毕业并被录取到清华大学计算机科学系。
2. 说明考入清华是很大的成绩。
3. 说明自己送给李朋的礼物——一张国航的往返机票。

参考范文

A Letter of Congratulation

Jan. 15, 2011

Dear Li Peng,

　　Congratulations on your graduation from high school with honors as well as your enrollment in the Computer Science Department of Tsinghua University. I know how hard you have been working and I am very proud of you for your achievement.

Tsinghua University is one of the most prestigious universities in China. Getting admitted to that university itself is a big accomplishment, not to mention to be accepted to the most competitive department — computer science.

Enclosed please find an Air China domestic roundtrip ticket, which is a gift from me upon your graduation. You can use it to fly to anywhere within China. I hope you would enjoy having a good summer vacation.

Again, my heartiest congratulations.

Affectionately,

Li Ming

（126 words）

一句话点评

在第一段中祝贺李朋时所说明的原因亲切自然，这是祝贺信的一个重要写作环节。

全文翻译

一封祝贺信

亲爱的李朋：

祝贺你高中毕业并且被清华大学计算机科学系录取。我知道你是多么的努力学习。我为你的成绩感到骄傲。

清华大学是中国最享有盛誉的大学之一。被录取到清华大学本身就是一个巨大的成就，更不要说被录取到最有竞争性的系——计算机科学系。

随信寄去国航国内往返机票一张，这是我给你的毕业礼物。你可以用这张票在国内飞行。我希望你将度过美好的暑期。

再一次表达我衷心的祝贺。

挚爱的

李明

2011 年 1 月 15 日

重点写作词语点睛

congratulation *n.* 祝贺	enrollment *n.* 入学
prestigious *a.* 享有声望的	enclosed *a.* 被附上的
roundtrip *a.* 来回旅程的	hearty *a.* 衷心的

写作题目与要求

Cui Wei, your friend, has won a speech contest. Write a letter to him to

1) express your congratulations on him and his performance, and

2) analyze the reason for his success.

You should write about 100 words on ANSWER SHEET 2. Do not sign your own name at the end of the letter. Use "Li Ming" instead. You do not need to write the address. (10 points)

具体写作思路

1. 对朋友获得演讲比赛的成功表示祝贺并夸奖他自然、流利和风趣，具体指明朋友的讲演五次被笑声和掌声所打断。

2. 说明巨大努力和聪明是朋友取得成功的原因。

参考范文

A Letter of Congratulation

Jan. 15, 2011

Dear Cui Wei,

Congratulations on your winning this year's speech contest! What a wonderful performance you gave yesterday! You were natural, fluent, and of course, humorous. Did you realize how much applause you earned at that time? Your speech was interrupted five times by laughter and applause from the audience. It was superb!

I am so happy for your success and I know more than anyone else how much effort you have put in the practice. Yes, you are talented, but it is your efforts that won you the top honor of the contest.

I just can't tell you how proud I feel of you.

Yours truly

Li Ming

(112 words)

一句话点评

在第一段中对朋友讲演的具体描述真切感人，这种写作方法是祝贺信所不可缺少的内容。

一封祝贺信

亲爱的崔伟：

祝贺你赢得今年的演讲比赛大奖。昨天你发挥的特别好！你表现得自然、流利并且风趣。你知道你赢得了多少掌声吗？你的讲演五次被笑声和掌声所打断。太棒了！

我为你的成功感到快乐。我比任何人都清楚你为之付出了多少努力。是的，你很聪明，但是你的努力才是你赢得比赛大奖的关键。

我无法用语言来表达我是多么的为你骄傲。

真挚的

李明

2011 年 1 月 15 日

重点写作词语点睛

contest *n*. 比赛	performance *n*. 表现
fluent *a*. 流利的	applause *n*. 鼓掌
interrupt *v*. 打断	talented *a*. 有才能的

考研英语应用文写作备考试题　　第 35 篇

写作题目与要求

Wang Lin, one of your high school classmates, has recently encountered some difficulties in his study. Write a letter to him to

1）state your own view on fate

2）offer possible example(s) about setbacks（挫折）before achieving success, and

3）describe positive effect of setbacks.

You should write about 100 words on ANSWER SHEET 2. Do not sign your own name at the end of the letter. Use "Li Ming" instead. You do not need to write the address.（10 points）

具体写作思路

1. 用"自助者上帝助之"这句名言表明自己对命运的看法。

2. 借用莱特兄弟的例子来说明不经风雨怎能见彩虹。

3. 用人们不珍惜轻易得来的成果这一普遍现象来反证失败所带来的正面作用。

A Letter of Encouragement

Jan. 15，2011

Dear Wang Lin,

I do believe that we make our own fate. As an English proverb goes, "God helps those who help themselves."

The most successful people in this world can not achieve their fame and popularity without getting knocked down a few times. The Wright brothers probably crashed their "flying machine" numerous times before achieving flight. The real test of a dream or ambition comes when it is most in danger of being snuffed.

Fighting through problems to achieve your dreams often sweetens success. Dreams that are too easily realized or goals that are achieved without any hardship often go unappreciated. Hold on and your tomorrow will be better.

Sincerely yours,

Li Ming

(114 words)

一句话点评

能够在写作中适当使用谚语或名人名言是取得写作高分的途径之一。

全文翻译

一封鼓励信

亲爱的王林：

我坚信命运掌握在我们自己手里。俗话说："自助者上帝助之"。

世界上最成功的人士都是遭受过命运打击之后才取得今天的名誉和知名度。莱特兄弟无数次的坠毁飞机之后才使飞机最后飞翔在蓝天。当梦想和抱负处于被扼杀的危险时，真正的考验才到来。

克服困难去努力实现你的梦想通常使成功更加甜美。不经过困难就轻易实现的梦想或者达到的目标通常不被人们所重视。如果你能坚持，你的明天会更好。

真诚的

李明

2011 年 1 月 15 日

重点写作词语点睛

fate　*n.* 命运

proverb　*n.* 俗语，常言

achieve　*v.* 达到，取得　　　　crash　*v.* 使(飞机等)坠毁(或撞坏)

snuff　*v.* 扼杀，消灭　　　　　hardship　*n.* 困苦，苦难

考研英语应用文写作备考试题　　第 36 篇

写作题目与要求

Zhang Hong, one of your university classmates, is seriously ill and hospitalized. Write a letter to

1) express your sorry to hear her bad news,

2) encourage her to overcome the illness, and

3) offer your help.

You should write about 100 words on ANSWER SHEET 2. Do not sign your own name at the end of the letter. Use "Li Ming" instead. You do not need to write the address. (10 points)

具体写作思路

1. 深切地表示很遗憾地听说张红生病住院。

2. 从张红是一个有信念的女孩、301 医院高超的治疗水平以及张红的精神状态等方面鼓励张红战胜疾病。

3. 具体表明自己将用发送手机短信的方式来帮助张红战胜疾病。

参考范文

A Letter of Consolation

Jan. 15, 2011

Dear Zhang Hong,

I am terribly sorry to hear that you are suddenly ill and hospitalized. I do feel much worried when I get to know that you received an operation last week.

I do hope that you have enough confidence to overcome the illness since in my mind you are always a girl of conviction. With the advanced medical facilities and experienced doctors in No. 301 People's Liberation Army Hospital, you will soon recover. Anyway, your state of mind and co-operation with doctors are of much importance.

From now on, I will send you text messages via mobile phone every day to give you spiritual support. I do hope that you will recover and come back soon.

Sincerely yours

Li Ming

(122 words)

文章第二段的叙述十分具体真实、层次鲜明，这是高分写作的最大特点。

全文翻译

一封慰问信

亲爱的张红：

我非常抱歉地听说你突然生病并且住院。当我得知你上星期接受手术时，我更感到担心。

我的确希望你有足够的信心来战胜疾病，因为在我心中你一直是一个有信念的女孩。有了301解放军医院先进的医疗设备和经验丰富的医生，你不久就会康复。无论如何，你的心情和与医生的配合是非常重要的。

从现在起，我将每天给你发手机短信以给你精神支持。我确信你不久就会康复并且回到我们当中。

真诚的

李明

2011 年 1 月 15 日

重点写作词语点睛

consolation	*n.* 慰问	operation	*n.* 手术
conviction	*n.* 信念	state of mind	思想状态
message	*n.* 信息	mobile phone	手机

考研英语应用文写作备考试题　　第 37 篇

写作题目与要求

Lu Yi, one of your best friends, is injured in a car accident. Write a letter to him to

1) express your reaction, and

2) suggest a safer way to travel in urban areas.

You should write about 100 words on ANSWER SHEET 2. Do not sign your own name at the end of the letter. Use "Li Ming" instead. You do not need to write the address. (10 points)

具体写作思路

1. 表达对朋友因车祸受伤而感到震惊，并表达听说伤势不严重而感到宽慰。

2. 建议最佳的交通方式是公共交通。

3. 表示希望朋友不久将康复。

A Letter of Consolation

Jan. 15, 2011

Dear Lu Yi,

You may never know how shocked I was to hear that you were injured in a car accident last Sunday. We were, however, a bit relieved to learn later on that the injury was a minor one and you are back home now.

Driving in the city is getting harder and harder particularly with those taxi drivers cutting into lanes and jumping red lights. The best way to travel in the city is to take mass transit— the bus and the subway. It is safe as well as fast.

I hope you will soon recover completely.

Yours sincerely

Li Ming

(106 words)

一句话点评

在第一段中对震惊和宽慰两种情感反映的描写对照性强烈，这是短文写作中难以写出的亮点。

全文翻译

一封慰问信

亲爱的陆毅：

你也许永远不会知道我听说你上周日在车祸中受伤时是多么地震惊。然而，后来我得知你的伤势不重并且现在已经回家时，我稍许感到宽慰。

在城市里开车越来越艰难了，尤其是那些出租车司机在车道上抢道并且闯红灯。在城市里最好的交通方式是利用公共交通 —— 公共汽车和地铁。这又安全又快捷。

我希望你不久将完全恢复。

真诚的

李明

2011 年 1 月 15 日

重点写作词语点睛

shock	*v.* 震惊	relieve	*v.* 使宽慰
minor	*a.* 较小的	lane	*n.* 车道
mass transit	公共交通	subway	*n.* 地铁

写作题目与要求

Hu Bing, one of your friends, failed in the last IELTS and is upset. Write a letter to him to

1）express your pity, point out the reason for his failure,

2）encourage him, and remind him of more important things to do.

You should write about 100 words on ANSWER SHEET 2. Do not sign your own name at the end of the letter. Use "Li Ming" instead. You do not need to write the address. （10 points）

具体写作思路

1. 明确表示对朋友雅思成绩不理想而感到遗憾，并且让他别泄气。指出其考试成绩不理想的原因是生病。告诉他还有机会考雅思，因为他现在上大一。

2. 提醒他不要耽误课业和期末考试。

参考范文

A Letter of Consolation

Jan. 15, 2011

Dear Hu Bing,

I am so sorry to learn of the unfortunate news that you didn't score very high on the last IELTS. I hope you won't feel too discouraged by the result. You know you could have done better had you not been sick during the test day, and you know there will always be another chance to take the IELTS. You are just a freshman now and you still have plenty of time to prepare for applying for admission to an American college.

For now, just forget about the test and cheer up. You have more important things to do, such as school work and final examinations.

If there is anything I can do, give me a call.

Yours,
Li Ming
（127 words）

一句话点评

在第一段中作者给出朋友应该振作的理由，所提到的两个具体理由十分真实，这是慰问信所不可缺少的要素。

一封慰问信

亲爱的胡兵：

　　我非常抱歉地得知上次雅思考试你的分数不高。我希望你不会因成绩而感到过于沮丧。你知道如果不是因为你考试的当天生病，你会考得更好。你还会有机会参加雅思考试的。你现在只是一个大一的学生，所以你有充分的时间准备申请美国的大学。

　　目前，一定要忘记这次考试并且振奋起来。你有更重要的事情要做，例如课业和期末考试。

　　如果有我能帮忙的，请打电话通知我。

你的
李明
2011 年 1 月 15 日

重点写作词语点睛

consolation	*n.* 慰问	IELTS	雅思
discourage	*v.* 使气馁	apply for	申请
admission	*n.* 入学	cheer up	振作

考研英语应用文写作备考试题　　第 39 篇

写作题目与要求

　　You will graduate from university and plan to hold a graduation party. Write an announcement to

　　1）state the time and venue of the party,

　　2）introduce what is to be done at the party, and

　　3）state the way to register.

　　You should write about 100 words on ANSWER SHEET 2. Do not sign your own name at the end of the announcement. Use "Li Ming" instead. You do not need to write the address. (10 points)

具体写作思路

　　1. 说明 2011 年 6 月 10 日晚在北京科技大学南区学术交流中心东宴会厅为 2010 届毕业生举行毕业典礼。

　　2. 说明领导、教师和外国专家将出席，从本校毕业的名人来讲演，师生共进晚餐。

3. 说明登记参加晚会的电话是 010-82073660。

参考范文

An Announcement

On the evening of June 10th, 2011, a grand graduation party for the 2010 graduates of Beijing University of Science and Technology is to be held in the East Banquet Hall of the Academic Exchange Center in the South District of our university.

All the seniors on the campus are warmly welcomed since this is your only opportunity to get together before graduation. Leaders, teachers, and foreigner experts of our university will show up at the party. What's more, some social celebrities who graduated from our university will come and make speeches. Teachers and students will dine together to celebrate the graduation day.

Any senior who intends to join the graduation party may register in advance via the phone number (010) 82073660.

Li Ming

(124 words)

一句话点评

本文在第一段中所交代的时间和地点十分具体、准确，这是通知类写作的关键。

全文翻译

通　　知

兹定于 2011 年 6 月 10 日晚在本校南区学术交流中心东宴会厅举行北京科技大学 2010 届毕业生盛大毕业派对。

欢迎我校所有大四的学生参加，因为这是毕业前你唯一的一次聚会机会。领导、老师和外国专家将光临派对。此外，我校毕业的一些社会名人将前来演讲。师生将共进晚餐庆祝毕业吉日。

欲参加毕业派对的大四学生可通过电话 010-82073660 提前登记。

李明

2011 年 1 月 15 日

重点写作词语点睛

announcement *n.* 通知	grand *a.* 盛大的
graduate *n.* 毕业生	banquet *n.* 宴会
celebrity *n.* 名人	register *v.* 登记

187

写作题目与要求

A basketball match is to be held between your university team and the Cambridge University Team tomorrow. However, the match can not come as scheduled. Write an announcement of sports delay to

1) announce the delay of the basketball match,

2) state the reason for the delay, and

3) announce the new date and venue of the match.

You should write about 100 words on ANSWER SHEET 2. Do not sign your own name at the end of the announcement. Use "Li Ming" instead. You do not need to write the address. (10 points)

具体写作思路

1. 以抱歉的方式通知将要推迟原定于明天举行的贵校与剑桥大学之间的篮球赛。

2. 说明推迟的原因是对方国家一直受大雾困扰，故飞机不能起飞。

3. 通知球赛改为下周六晚七点，地点不变。

参考范文

An Announcement

Jan. 15, 2011

Dear Teachers and Schoolmates,

We feel terribly sorry to inform all of you that the basketball match between our university team and the Cambridge University Team which is scheduled to be held tomorrow has to be delayed.

The Cambridge University Team should arrive at our university in the afternoon. However, these days, the United Kingdom has been shrouded in thick fog and the visibility is rather poor so that all the airports have been closed and the Cambridge University Team is prevented from coming to our university.

Through our mutual contact, the basketball match is delayed to 7:00 p. m. next Sunday at the same venue.

Li Ming

(105 words)

一句话点评

第二段中所给山的原因十分具体且真实，写作内容的具体和真实性是夺取高分的一个重要途径。

全文翻译

通　知

亲爱的老师和同学们：

　　我抱歉地通知大家，原定于明天的我校和剑桥大学之间的篮球赛因故延迟。

　　剑桥大学队应在今天下午到达我校。然而，近来，英国一直受浓雾困扰并且能见度十分低，以至于所有机场关闭，剑桥大学队来我校受阻。

　　经相互联系，篮球赛被推迟到下周六晚七点，地点不变。

李明

2011 年 1 月 15 日

重点写作词语点睛

inform sb. of　告知某人某事	schedule　*v.* 安排
delay　*v.* 延迟	shroud　*v.* 覆盖；掩蔽
mutual　*a.* 相互的	venue　*n.* 地点

考研英语应用文写作备考试题　　第 41 篇

写作题目与要求

An annual English essay contest is to be held by Students' Union. As organizer of the event, write an announcement to

1）state the basic requirements,

2）clarify the way to publicize the result, and

3）inform the public of the deadline for entering the contest.

You should write about 100 words on ANSWER SHEET 2. Do not sign your own name at the end of the announcement. Use "Li Ming" instead. （10 points）

具体写作思路

1. 明确告知参赛者只能交一篇文章参赛，要正规打印，来稿不退，去掉任何识别标记，填写参赛表格并且和文章装订在一起，将参赛文章交系学生会主席。

2. 告知比赛成绩将于 2011 年春季学期通知参赛者。

3. 告知截止日期是 2011 年 2 月 17 日。

参考范文

An Announcement

Jan. 15, 2011

Students' Union of Peking University announces the rules for <u>entering</u> the contest of the fourth English Essay Contest

1. You may enter only one essay. Type the essay you enter, <u>double-spaced</u>, on standard typing paper. Essays can not be returned. Remove all <u>identification</u> from the essay. Fill out the entry form and <u>staple</u> it to the front of your essay. Give the essay to president of Students' Union of your department. He will enter it in the contest for you.

2. Winners will be <u>notified</u> before the end of the Spring <u>term</u>, 2011. Prizes will be similar to those listed in this year's *Guide to Composition*.

3. The <u>deadline</u> for entering the contest is February 17, 2011.

Students' Union
(119 words)

一句话点评

本文对大赛的参赛细则交代得十分具体，这正是通知类写作的重要特点。

全文翻译

通　　知

北京大学学生会有关第四届英语作文大赛参赛规则的通知：

一、参赛者只能呈交一篇文章参赛，需将参赛文章隔行打印在标准打印纸张上。来稿不退。请消除文章中一切识别标记。填写参赛表格并将表格装订在参赛文章的前面。请将参赛文章交本系学生会主席，他将为你交稿参赛。

二、在 2011 年春季学期结束之前将通知获奖者。奖励办法与本年度《写作指导》中所列举的一样。

三、大赛交稿截止日期为 2011 年 2 月 17 日。

2011 年 1 月 15 日

重点写作词语点睛

announcement　*n*. 通知	enter　*v*. 递呈
double-space　（在打字机上）隔行打	identification　*n*. 辨认；识别
staple　*v*. 订	notify　*v*. 通知
term　*n*. 学期	deadline　*n*. 截止日期

190

写作题目与要求

You intend to improve your English with the help of foreign friends. You plan to look for a foreigner who intends to learn Chinese so that you can exchange lessons. Write a notice to

1）briefly introduce yourself and purpose,

2）depict profile of the foreigner you intend to exchange your lesson with, and

3）offer your way of contact.

You should write about 100 words on ANSWER SHEET 2. Do not sign your own name at the end of the notice. Use "Li Ming" instead. You do not need to write the address. (10 points)

具体写作思路

1. 以一名大四学生的身份来说明自己想要提高口语并寻找外国人帮助的目的。

2. 提出你要寻找的外国人可以和你交换课程、他应符合是本土美国人、大学毕业生、学语言学等要求。

3. 说明自己的联系手机号码是 13801225270。

参考范文

A Notice

I, the undersigned, am a senior in the Computer Science Department of Peking University. I would like to sharpen my English speaking skills so that I write the notice to look for a foreigner for help.

Since I am a student and do not have my own income, I would like to look for a foreigner who wants to learn Chinese and exchange language lessons with me. The foreigner must be native American and college graduate. What's more, his/her major should be linguistics.

Any foreigner who is interested in the exchange of language learning may reach me via the mobile phone number 13801225270.

Li Ming

(105 words)

一句话点评

在第二段对于外国人的要求写的准确、具体，这是启事类写作必不可少的特点。

启　事

我是北京大学计算机科学系一名大四的学生。我想要提高英语口语，故发此启事以寻找外国人帮助。

由于本人是学生无收入，故想寻找一位欲学汉语能和我交换课程的外国人。该人必须是美国人、大学生。此外，其专业必须是语言学。

对交换课程有兴趣的任何外国人可通过手机电话13801225270和我联系。

李明

重点写作词语点睛

sharpen	*v.* 加强	notice	*n.* 启事
native	*a.* 本土的，本国人	major	*n.* 专业
linguistics	*n.* 语言学	via	*prep.* 通过

考研英语应用文写作备考试题　　第43篇

写作题目与要求

You will graduate from university next summer and have a lot of old reference books to sell. Write a notice of sales to

1）state the reason for sales,

2）introduce the old reference books, and

3）your way of contact.

You should write about 100 words on ANSWER SHEET 2. Do not sign your own name at the end of the notice. Use "Li Ming" instead. You do not need to write the address. （10 points）

具体写作思路

1. 说明自己将要毕业，故要把旧书卖掉。

2. 说明旧书涉及生物、天文、数学、四六级和考研。

3. 告知自己的联系电话是手机13801225270。

参考范文

A Notice

I, the undersigned, am a senior in the Computer Science Department of Tsinghua University. I will graduate next summer so that I write the notice to <u>sell</u> some of my old reference books.

My old reference books will be sold at <u>incredible</u> <u>discount</u>. My books <u>cover</u> several scientific fields including biology, astronomy, and mathematics. Some of the books are written by world famous scientists like Dr. Hawking. What's more, English books on CET 4, CET 6, and NETEM are also available. Most of them contain the lastest <u>genuine</u> test papers. Most importantly, my valuable in-class <u>notes</u> are on the books.

Anyone who is interested in my old books may contact me. I can be reached via the phone number 13801225270.

Li Ming

（120 words）

一句话点评

在第二段中对所卖书籍的介绍非常详细，并告知折扣很大，这种写作方法恰恰是启事的必备要素。

全文翻译

启　　事

我是清华大学计算机科学系一名大四学生。今年夏天我将毕业，故发此启事以变卖本人的旧书。

我的旧书将以令人难以置信的折扣出售。我的旧书涉及若干科学领域，包括生物学、天文学和数学。一些书籍的作者是世界著名科学家，例如霍金。此外，还有四六级和考研英语书。大多数书包含最新真题。重要的是，书上还有宝贵的课堂笔记。

对我的旧书感兴趣的人可以和我联系。我的手机号码是 13801225270。

李明

重点写作词语点睛

sell　*v.* 出售	incredible　*a.* 令人难以置信的
discount　*n.* 折扣	cover　*v.* 涉及
genuine　*a.* 真的	note　*n.* 笔记

考研英语应用文写作备考试题　　第 44 篇

写作题目与要求

You have found an electronic dictionary and want to return it to its owner. Write a notice of Lost and Found to clearly state：

    1）the time and place of your finding

    2）the feature of the dictionary，and

    3）your information for contact.

You should write about 100 words on ANSWER SHEET 2. Do not sign your own name at the end of the notice. Use "Li Ming" instead. You do not need to write the address.（10 points）

具体写作思路

1. 具体交代 2011 年 1 月 4 日晚你在本校东区新图书馆三层英语阅览室捡到一个电子辞典。

2. 说明电子辞典的特点如下：崭新、金属灰色、小蛋糕大小、像普通杂志一样厚。

3. 交代自己的联系电话是 010-62043340 和 13801225270。

参考范文

Lost and Found

On the evening of January 4th，2011，I found an electronic dictionary in the English reading-room on the 3rd floor of the new library in the east district of our university.

The electronic dictionary can be generally described as follows. It is brand new and metallic gray in color. What's more, the portable electronic dictionary is as big as a piece of cake and as thin as a regular magazine.

The owner of the electronic dictionary may contact me now. My room phone number and mobile phone number are（010）62043340 and 13801225270 respectively. Please make an appointment in advance.

Li Ming

（102 words）

一句话点评

对捡到物品的时间、地点的描述十分具体准确，这是失物招领启事类写作的核心元素。

全文翻译

失物招领启事

2011 年 1 月 4 日晚，本人在本校东区新图书馆三层的英语阅览室捡到一本电子辞典。

电子辞典可简要描述如下。这是一个崭新的辞典，金属灰色。此外，这个轻便的电子辞典和一块普通的蛋糕一样大小，和普通的杂志薄厚一样。

电子辞典的主人可以和我联系。我的房间电话和移动电话分别是 010-62043340 和 13801225270。请提前约定。

李明

重点写作词语点睛

metallic	*a.* 金属的	portable	*a.* 轻便的
contact	*v.* 联系	respectively	*ad.* 分别地
appointment	*n.* 约会	in advance	事先

考研英语应用文写作备考试题　　第 45 篇

写作题目与要求

Ms. Smith wrote to you, claiming that there was something wrong with her heating system. As building supervisor, write a note to Ms. Smith to

1）inform her of her heating system check-up, and

2）express apology for the inconvenience.

You should write about 100 words on ANSWER SHEET 2. Do not sign your own name at the end of the note. Use "Li Ming" instead. You do not need to write the address. (10 points)

具体写作思路

1. 通知史密斯女士热力系统已经检查，发现必须更换，明后天不能供暖，但周末寒流到来前可恢复正常。

2. 对由此带来的不便深感歉意。

参考范文

A Note

Jan. 15, 2011

Dear Ms. Smith,

Thanks for your letter about the heating. We have had a plumber check the system today and we were told that the system was too old and that it had to be replaced. The contractor will send workers to install a new furnace the day after tomorrow. So for today and tomorrow there will be no heat for the entire building, but please rest assured that the new heating system will work before the cold front arrives this weekend.

We apologize for the inconvenience. And we value your understanding and cooperation.

Li Ming

Building Supervisor

(101 words)

在第一段有关热力系统的故障检查以及系统恢复的交代简明扼要、层次鲜明，这是短笺类写作的普遍特色。

全文翻译

便　　笺

亲爱的史密斯女士：

感谢您有关热力系统的来信。我们已经让水暖工检查了该系统，我们被告知该系统太陈旧了需要替换。承包商将在后天派工人安装一个新锅炉。所以今明两天整幢楼无法供暖。但是请放心在本周末寒流到来之前新的热力系统将投入运行。

我们对由此带来的不便深表歉意。我们珍视您的理解和合作。

李明

楼房监管员

2011 年 1 月 15 日

重点写作词语点睛

note　 *n.* 短笺，便条	plumber　 *n.* 水暖工
contractor　 *n.* 承包人，承包商	install　 *v.* 安装
furnace　 *n.* 炉子	rest assured that …　 放心
cold front　 寒流	inconvenience　 *n.* 不方便

考研英语应用文写作备考试题　　第 46 篇

写作题目与要求

A luncheon is to be held on February 6th, 2011 to welcome Prof. William. As a conference coordinator, write a memo to Dr. David Smith to

1）remind him of the luncheon, and

2）confirm the time and venue.

You should write about 100 words on ANSWER SHEET 2. Do not sign your own name at the beginning of the memo. Use "Li Ming" instead. （10 points）

具体写作思路

1. 提醒大卫·史密斯博士出席为欢迎汤姆·威廉教授及其代表团而举行的午餐会。

2. 通知时间是 2011 年 2 月 6 日，地点在本校东区国际学术交流中心的宴会厅。

A Memo

To：Dr. David Smith

From：Li Ming

Ref：<u>Luncheon</u> to Welcome Professor William

Date：February 3rd，2011

This is a <u>reminder</u> of the invitation to a luncheon to welcome Professor Tom William and his delegation of senior professors and researchers from New York University to the Computer Science and Technology Department of Tsinghua University. During the luncheon，Professor William will make a <u>presentation</u> to the students and teachers from the colleges and universities in Beijing.

The luncheon is <u>scheduled</u> for Tuesday，February 6th，2011，at 12 a. m. ，at the <u>Banquet Hall</u> of the International <u>Academic Exchanges</u> Center on East Campus.　　　　(100 words)

一句话点评

本文对时间、地点和相关事宜的交代十分准确，这是备忘录写作的重要特点。

全文翻译

备　忘　录

致：大卫·史密斯博士

来自：李明

有关：欢迎威廉教授的午餐会

时间：2011 年 2 月 3 日

这里谨提醒邀请您出席为欢迎汤姆·威廉教授及其代表团而举行的午餐会。他及其代表团来清华大学计算机科学系访问。该代表团由老教授和研究人员组成。午餐会上，威廉教授将向来自于北京高校的教师和学生进行介绍。

午餐会定于 2011 年 2 月 6 日（星期二）中午 12 点在东区国际学术交流中心宴会厅举行。

重点写作词语点睛

memo	*n.* 备忘录	luncheon	*n.* 午餐会
reminder	*n.* 提示	presentation	*n.* 陈述
schedule	*v.* 计划	Banquet Hall	宴会厅
academic exchange	学术交流		

写作题目与要求

Xuezi Apartment is now under annual repair and overhaul. As domestic administrator, write a memo to

1）inform all residents of the undergoing work, and

2）suggest a choice concerning lodging for the residents.

You should write about 100 words on ANSWER SHEET 2. Do not sign your own name at the beginning of the memo. Use "Li Ming" instead. （10 points）

具体写作思路

1. 通知学子楼的居住者：本楼盥洗室进行每年一次的维修，下周四可正常使用。
2. 建议在此期间想到主楼居住的人与林女士联系。

参考范文

A Memo

To：All Residents of Xuezi Apartment

From：The Domestic Administrator

Ref：Bathroom and Toilet Repairs

Date：February 3rd, 2011

　　Owing to the annual repairs and overhaul being completed in the bathrooms and toilets in Xuezi Apartment, it would be helpful if residents did not use them for a few days. Hopefully the facilities should be ready by next Thursday, but to have a completely satisfactory job done, the floors MUST NOT BE WALKED ON for 24 hours at least.

　　If any resident would like to sleep in the main hall during this period, he may contact Ms. Lin on Monday, February 5th. 　　　　　　　　　　　　　　　　（102 words）

一句话点评

本文写作语言简练、重点突出，这正是备忘录类写作所要求的写作方式。

全文翻译

备　忘　录

致：学子公寓的所有居住者

来自：校内管理员

有关：盥洗室的维修

日期：2011 年 2 月 3 日

　　由于学子楼盥洗室每年一度的维修正在进行之中，本楼居住者近几日暂不能使用相关设施。相关设施预计在下周四可以使用。但是，为了保证工作的圆满，至少在 24 小时内不要在地板上随意走动。

　　在此期间，本楼任何欲想在主楼居住者，可以在 2 月 5 日（星期一）与林女士联系。

重点写作词语点睛

apartment　　*n.* 公寓　　　　administrator　　*n.* 管理人

facility　　*n.* 设施　　　　　resident　　*n.* 居住者

main hall　　主楼

考研英语应用文写作备考试题　　第 48 篇

写作题目与要求

Many people have called to ask for directions on how to get to a conference to be held next week. As a conference coordinator, write directions

　　1）for those who take public transportation（bus and subway）, and

　　2）for private car drivers and bicycle riders.

You should write about 100 words on ANSWER SHEET 2. Do not sign your own name at the end of your directions. Use "Li Ming" instead. You do not need to write the address.（10 points）

具体写作思路

　　1. 明确告知乘公共汽车的人应选择 43 路公共汽车或地铁到蓝天站下车；自己开车或骑自行车的人走三环，东四大街右拐，向西走三公里后到育林大街，然后左拐。

　　2. 留联系电话。

参考范文

Directions

Jan. 15, 2011

Dear Sir or Madam,

　　Many of you have called to ask for directions on how to get to the <u>conference</u> to be held at Beijing Normal University. Here are the <u>directions</u>.

　　For those taking public transportation：

　　Take Bus No. 43 to its <u>terminal</u> station; or take <u>subway</u> to Blue Sky Station and walk west for about 10 minutes.

For those driving or riding a bicycle:

Take Third Ring Road to the south, turn right at Dong Si Avenue, travel for about 3 kilometers to the west, and you will come up to Yulin Street. Turn left at Yulin Street, and you will see the main gate of the university.

There will be <u>signs</u> at the university entrance to lead you to the <u>auditorium</u> where the conference is held.

If you have any further difficulty, please feel free to call me at (010) 82073660.

Sincerely yours,

Li Ming

Conference Coordinator

(151 words)

一句话点评

本文把公共交通等线路描述的非常具体，这种交代方法是指导类写作所不可缺少的写作方法。

全文翻译

路 线 指 引

亲爱的女士/先生：

许多人打来电话询问有关到达北京师范大学举办会议场地的交通路线。下面是交通指引：

乘坐公共交通的人：

可乘 43 路公共汽车到达终点站下车；或乘地铁在蓝天车站下车并向西走大约十分钟。

自己驾车或骑自行车者：

沿三环向南，在东四大街右拐，向西约三公里，便是育林大街。在育林大街左拐，你就看到师大的主门。

在学校的门口会有标志引领你到举行会议的礼堂。

如果你还有问题，请拨 (010) 82073660 与我联系。

真诚的

李明

会议协调员

2011 年 1 月 15 日

重点写作词语点睛

conference n. 会议	direction n. 指导
terminal n. 终点站	subway n. 地铁
sign n. 标志	auditorium n. 礼堂

写作题目与要求

Read the following text carefully and write an abstract of it in 80—100 words. You should write your abstract on ANSWER SHEET 2. (10 points)

How New York Became America's Largest City

In the 19th century New York was smaller than Philadelphia and Boston. Today it is the largest city in America. How can the change in its size and importance be explained?

To answer this question we must consider certain facts about geography, history, and economics. Together these three will explain the huge growth of American's most famous city.

The map of the Northeast shows that four of the most heavily populated areas in this region are around seaports. At these points materials from across the sea enter the United States, and the products of the land are sent there for export across the sea.

Economists know that places where transportation lines meet are good places for making raw materials into finished goods. That is why seaports often have cities nearby. But cities like New York needed more than their geographical location in order to become great industrial centers. Their development did not happen simply by chance.

About 1815, when many Americans from the east coast had already moved toward the west, trade routes from the ports to the central regions of the country began to be a serious problem. The slow wagons of that time, drawn by horses or oxen, were too expensive for moving heavy freight very far. Americans had long admired Europe's canals. In New York State, a canal seemed the best solution to the transportation problem. From the eastern end of Lake Erie all the way across the state to the Hudson River there is a long strip of low land. Here the Erie Canal was constructed. After several years of work it was completed in 1825.

The canal produced an immediate effect. Freight costs were cut to about one-tenth of what they had been. New York City, which had been smaller than Philadelphia and Boston, quickly became the leading city on the coast. In the years that followed, transportation routes on the Great Lakes were joined to routes on the Mississippi River. Then New York City became the end point of a great inland shipping system that extended from the Atlantic Ocean far up the western branches of the Mississippi.

The coming of the railroads made canal shipping less important, but it ties New York even more closely to the central regions of the country. It was easier for people in the central states to ship their goods to New York for export overseas.

Exports from New York were greater than imports. Consequently, shipping companies were eager to fill their ships with passengers on the return trip from Europe. Passengers could come from Europe very cheaply as a result.

Thus New York became the greatest port for receiving people from European countries. Many of these people remained in the city. Others stayed in New York for a few weeks, months or years, and then moved to other parts of the United States. For these great numbers of new Americans New York had to provide homes, goods and services. Their labor helped the city to become great.

具体写作思路

1. 归纳纽约靠近海港的地理优势作用。
2. 归纳出 the Erie Canal 在水路交通方面的作用。
3. 归纳出铁路运输的作用。
4. 归纳出来自于欧洲的人们对纽约发展所起的作用。

参考范文

Abstract

New York was once smaller than Philadelphia and Boston, but now it is America's largest city because of geography, history and economics.

New York is around a seaport where materials were imported to the US and the products of the US were sent abroad across the sea. The city was further developed when the Erie Canal was completed in 1825. This linked Lake Erie to New York via the Hudson River, and the cost of transporting goods to the inland was cut down. In addition, the Great Lakes were soon linked to the Mississippi. Later, railroads tied New York even closer to the central states, whose goods were exported via New York. Fewer goods were imported, so cheap passages were available from Europe. New York became the main port for receiving Europeans, many of whom stayed in the city and helped it become America's largest city.　　(139 words)

一句话点评

本文摘要抓住了原文历史发展脉络中的重大事件。这种捕捉重要事件和作用的能力是摘要写作成功的法宝。

全文翻译

摘　要

纽约曾经比费城和波士顿还小，但是由于它的地理、历史和经济的原因，现在纽约是美国最大的城市。

202

纽约位于海港地区。在过去原料从这里输入美国，美国产品从这里运到海外。当伊利运河在 1825 年完工的时候，纽约进一步发展。运河经哈德逊河把伊利湖和纽约连接起来，这大大减少了将货物运到美国中部的成本。此外，五大湖不久就和密西西比河连接起来。后来，铁路把纽约和中部各州连接的更加紧密，这些州通过纽约把货物运到国外。由于美国从外国进口的货物不多，所以人们能够以低廉的价格乘坐美国出口货物的返航船只从欧洲来到美国。纽约成为接收欧洲人的主要港口，许多人在此逗留帮助纽约成为美国最大的城市。

重点写作词语点睛

geography	*n.* 地理		canal	*n.* 运河	
via	*prep.* 通过		cut down	减少	
tie	*v.* 连接		passage	*n.* 航行	

考研英语应用文写作备考试题　　第 50 篇

写作题目与要求

Study the following essay carefully and write an abstract of it in about 80—100 words. You should write your summary on ANSWER SHEET 2. （10 points）

Student Rights

Who knows better than the students themselves what a university should do for them and how they should be treated? Yet how often do students have any say at all in such important issues as faculty selection, curriculum planning, and scheduling? The answer is obvious: never. If university administrations refuse to include student representatives in the decision-making process, something drastic must be done.

Let's examine what is happening right here on our own campus in the areas mentioned above. The first major issue is the selection of faculty members. Never in the history of this college has a student been permitted to interview, examine the credentials of, or even meet prospective professors. All hiring is done by a joint administrative-faculty committee, often made up of people who will not even have extensive dealings with the individuals after they begin teaching. Those who have the most at stake and whose lives and academic careers will be governed by the professors—the students themselves—never even meet the new teachers until the first class meeting. No one is better equipped to evaluate a professor's ability to communicate with students than those whom he or she intends to teach. Anyone can read a curriculum vitae to ascertain the level of professional training and experience someone has had, but the best judges of a teacher's ability to teach, which is the primary function of any professor, are undoubtedly the students themselves.

Students' interest in and commitment to appropriate curricula are even more obvious.

We have come to college with very specific purposes in mind: to prepare ourselves intellectually and practically for the future. We know what we need to learn in order to compete successfully with others in our chosen fields. Why should we be kept out of the curriculum planning process? If we pay for the textbooks, spend hours in the library doing research, and burn the midnight oil studying for tests and exams, why are we not permitted to give our opinions about the materials we will spend so many hours studying? It is imperative that our views be made known to curriculum planners.

Finally, the area of scheduling is of vital interest to students. The hours at which classes are offered affect the workings of our daily lives. Many of us must juggle work and class schedules, but often administrators ignore such problems when they schedule classes. Schedules must be convenient and flexible so that all students have equal opportunities to take the most popular classes and those which are most essential to their majors. If students helped with scheduling, never would there be two required courses offered at the same time for only one semester per academic year. Never would we have to wait two or three semesters to take a course that is a prerequisite for other desired courses, nor would we have to race across campus in ten minutes to get from one class to the next. Students are vitally concerned with the scheduling area.

In the 1960s and early 1970s, students were not too shy or fearful to demonstrate against the injustices they saw in the draft system and the Vietnam conflict. Why should students today be afraid to voice their opinions about the very important issues that affect their very lives? It is imperative that students act to protect their own rights. Fellow university students, I urge that you meet together and draw up demands to be presented to the administration. We must take the future in our own hands, not be led to it like passive sheep. Let us act now so that we will not be sorry later!

具体写作思路

1. 总结归纳出学生有权利参与学校管理决策这一中心思想。
2. 总结归纳出学生应该参与决策的三个方面：教师选派、课程制订和上课规划。
3. 总结归纳出学生应该参加决策的两点理由：相关决策与学生有直接的利害关系；学生有做出明智决定的亲身经历。
4. 总结归纳出本文作者强烈呼吁学生们参与学校的管理决策。

参考范文

Abstract

Students have the right to be involved in university <u>administrative</u> decisions. Students should be included in decisions regarding selection of <u>faculty</u>, <u>curriculum</u> planning, and scheduling of classes. Students not only have more vital interests in the decisions made in these areas than those who traditionally settle the issues, but that they are also better equipped through their experiences as students to make <u>intelligent</u> decisions about them. It is <u>crucial</u> for students to become actively involved in protesting <u>unilateral</u> administrative decisions and it is high time that they met to discuss their mutual interests and demands.　　　（100 words）

一句话点评

　　本文摘要抓住了原文主旨思想并且把原文中的因果论证关系阐述得简洁清晰。这种写作特点恰恰是摘要所必须具备的。

全文翻译

摘　　要

　　学生有权利参与大学管理决策。他们应该被融入有关教师选派、课程规划和课堂计划等决策之中。与那些一直处理这些问题的人士相比，学生不仅和这些方面的决策有着更大的利害关系，还更加具备通过自己的经历做出明智决策的能力。重要的是学生们要积极参与到反对单方面做出管理决策的行动中来。现在是大家一起讨论相互利益和要求的时候了。

重点写作词语点睛

administrative　*a*. 管理的	faculty　*n*. 教师
curriculum　*n*. 课程	intelligent　*a*. 明智的
crucial　*a*. 重要的	unilateral　*a*. 单方面的

读者意见反馈表

尊敬的读者，高等教育出版社出版的考研系列用书一直凭借其权威性和高质量深受广大考生的信赖。2011 年版考研系列辅导用书在内容组织、知识点编排、表述方式等方面做了改革和创新，目的就是希望高教版考研用书能够更加贴近考试实际、更加利于复习备考。但这个目标是否已达到还有待于您的评判。诚请您贡献出聪明才智，对如何完善考研系列用书献计献策，以便我们能更好地为您和其他考生服务。您的建议一经采纳，我们将给予奖励。

姓名：　　　联系方式：　　　　　地址：　　　　　邮编：　　　E-mail：

1. 您通过何种途径了解高教版考研用书：□书名　□网络　□朋友推荐　□广告　□其他_____

2. 您买了如下考研系列用书中的哪几本：政治：□大纲　□分析　□大纲解析　□全国考研辅导班系列（基础复习全书、大纲配套 1600 题、冲刺串讲）英语：□大纲　□分析　□大纲解析　□名师导学（真题、阅读、完型与写作、冲刺预测试卷）　□全国考研辅导班系列（真题考点透析、写作 100 篇、读真题记单词、全真冲刺）　数学：□大纲　□分析　□大纲解析　法律硕士：□大纲　□分析　□教育学大纲解析　□心理学大纲解析　□计算机基础综合大纲解析　管理类（MBA、BPA、MPAcc）：□考试大纲　□大纲解析　□全真冲刺试卷　□英语阅读理解　□逻辑　□写作　□英语（二）冲刺试卷

3. 影响您选择考研用书的因素：□内容质量　□权威性　□价格　□出版社名气　□作者名气　□早上市　□大纲出版后上市

4. 您认为高教版考研用书的定价：□过低　□略低　□适当　□略高　□过高

您认为合适的定价是多少（以一本书为例）：

5. 您认为辅导书最适宜的篇幅：□30 万字以内　□30 万 ~ 40 万字　□40 万 ~ 50 万字　□50 万字以上

6. 您更喜欢哪类考研用书：□基础类　□提高类　□专项训练类　□模拟试卷类　□重点精讲类

7. 何种促销活动更吸引您？□展销打折　□考研名师现场指导签名　□网络增值服务　□其他

8. 市场上现有考研图书最令您满意的是：_____

9. 您最喜欢的作者是谁？_____

10. 您在复习时常遇到哪方面困扰您的问题？_____

11. 您希望再编写什么方面的辅导书？_____

12. 现有考研图书需在哪些方面改进？_____

（如内容不敷填写可附页）

您也可以通过登录"中国教育考试在线"网站（www.eduexam.com.cn）提出您宝贵的意见，或将本页寄至"北京市朝阳区惠新东街 4 号富盛大厦 12 层考试分社，邮编 100029"。

郑 重 声 明